Ninja Foodi XL Pro Air Oven Cookbook for Beginners

150 Easy, Mouthwatering and Crispy Recipes to Feed Your Family Healthy with Your Favorite XL Pro Air Fry Oven

Adele T. Jorns

Table of Contents

Introduction

As per the trend, there are various digitally controlled multipurpose cooking appliances available in the market. Instead of finding multipurpose cooking appliance, find perfect cooking gadgets which are suitable as per your daily kitchen needs. Here in this book, we have used such a multipurpose appliance equipped with advanced technology to make your daily cooking process easy.

The Ninja Foodi XL Pro Air Oven is designed to cook a large portion of foods in a single cooking cycle. It is basically the combination of three different cooking techniques such as air fryer, toaster, and oven. The Ninja foodi XL oven has a multi-functional appliance capable to perform 10 1 cooking operations like air roast, air fry, whole roast, broil, reheat, toast, bake, dehydrate, bagel and pizza. The display comes with a big handle design offers a simple and user-friendly interface. The true surround convection technology cooks your food faster and gives you crispy and brown results without flipping or shaking the cooking basket. Compare to other countertop oven Ninja foodi XL cooks your food 30 % faster.

The book includes 100 different types of recipes like breakfast, poultry, beef, pork and lamb, fish and seafood, vegetables & side dishes, snacks & appetizer, dehydrate, and desserts. All the recipes written in this book are unique and written in an easily understandable form. The recipes are written in the standard format with their perfect preparation and cooking time followed by step by step cooking instructions. All the recipes end with their nutritional value information. This nutritional value information will help you to track the daily calories intake information. The book also comes with a 30-days meal plan. Meal planning will help you how much you have eating also prevent you from overeating. It saves your time, money, and avoids wasting foods. There are few books available in the market on this topic thanks for choosing my book. I hope you love and enjoy all the recipes written in this cookbook.

Chapter 1: Ninja Foodi XL Pro Air Oven Basics

Ninja Foodi XL Pro Air Oven

Ninja foodi XL pro air oven is another member comes from the Ninja family. Ninja foodi is leading manufacturers of high quality and innovative appliances. The Ninja foodi XL pro is one of the advanced cooking appliances made up of a combination of two different cooking techniques like convection, toaster, and air fryer. It comes in extra-large size and capable to cook 12 people's food within a single cooking cycle. It has a capacity to cook 5 lb of chicken, 12 lb turkey, a sheet pan of vegetable, and two large 12-inch size pizza.

The Ninja foodi XL pro air oven is loaded with true surround convection technology. It is capable to provide 10 times more convection power than a traditional convection oven and gives you faster cooking results. It not only cooks your food faster but also makes your food crispy from the outside and tender juicy from the inside. The Ninja foodi Xl requires 75 % less oil compared to the traditional air frying method. Ninja foodi XL pro air oven is one of the multi-functional versatile cooking appliances comes with 10 different cooking functions. These functions include Air fry, bake, broil, pizza, air roast, whole roast, bagel, toast, reheat and dehydrate. It works on 1800 watt power and prepares your meal 30 % faster compared to other full-size traditional ovens. The best part of the oven is that it takes just 90 seconds to preheat the oven. It is also capable to cook two cook your food into two levels and gives you even cooking results even without rotating the food.

The oven comes with a big digital display handle and the current working function illuminates gives an attractive design to the oven. If you accidentally open the door during the cooking process the current working program automatically freezes by the oven to prevent accidental changes happens in the cooking cycle. It is one of the perfect advanced cooking ovens available in the market which gives 30 % crispier results and 50 % more even baking results compare to other countertop ovens.

Functions of Ninja Foodi XL Pro Air Oven

The Ninja Foodi XL oven loaded with 10 in 1 different cooking functions. These functions are given as follows:

1. Whole Roast

Roasting will help to enhance the flavor, taste, and texture of your food. This function allows you to roast a large piece of meat, chicken, ham, Pork tenderloins, etc. along with potatoes or vegetables at a time. It has a capacity to roast 5 lb of chicken or 12 lb of turkey in a single cooking cycle. It makes your food nice crispy from the outside and juicy tender from the inside.

2. Air Roast

This function allows you to cook sheet pan meals like a thicker piece of chicken or meat along with veggies. Using this function you can air a roast lot of vegetables in a single cooking cycle. It gives the same cooking results as the whole roast function. Air Roast not only cooks your meal faster but also make it nice crispy from the outside and juicy and tender from the inside.

3. Air Fry

This function is used to frying your food with a nice golden brown texture like deep-fried food. Using this function you can fry your favorite food like French fries, chicken nuggets, bacon, pork chops, chicken wings, etc. within little oil or sometimes no oil. Like another countertop oven, you never need to shake or rearrange the food basket while cooking and you will get even cooking results.

4. Bake

Using this function you can bake your favorite cake, muffins, cookies, bread, and lots of dishes that come under this category. The Ninja Foodi XL is capable of gives a nice golden brown texture over your backed goods and you will get even cooking results every time.

5. Dehydrate

Dehydrating is one of the best ways to preserve your food for a long time. Using this function you can easily convert your fruits and vegetable slices into tasty, healthy, and delicious snacks. It is one of the long processes to dehydrate your food because the dehydrating process is done at low temperature for a long time period.

6. Broil

Broiling is one of the methods in which foods are exposed to direct radiant heat. Using this function you can easily brown top of the casseroles, broil fish, meat, nachos, and steak. You can finish broiling your food with crispy and golden brown texture over your food.

7. Toast

This function is used to toast your bread. Due to large cooking capacity, your Ninja Foodi XL air oven is capable to toast 9 slice of bread perfectly in a single toasting cycle. To use this function you have to choose the function first then select the number of slice you want to toast and the darkness level.

8. Bagel

Bagel is a doughnut-shaped thicker piece of bread. It takes a long time to toast like bread. While using this function the heat comes from the top and bottom side of food so it makes your bagel crisp on both top and bottom sides.

9. Pizza

Using this function you can make 12-inch size 2 pizzas at the same time. It makes your pizza crispy and golden. Making golden spots over pizza by melting and browning the cheese toppings. You can also use this function to reheat your leftover pizza and make it nice crispy and golden again.

10. Reheat

Using this function you can easily reheat your leftover food. The Ninja foodi XL evenly heat your food from the top and bottom side to make your food crisp from outside and tender from inside.

Benefits of Ninja Foodi XL Pro Air oven

The Ninja Foodi XL oven is loaded with various benefits these benefits are given as follows:

- Multi-cooking Appliances

The Ninja food XL pro air oven is loaded with 10 different cooking functions in one appliance. You never need to buy separate appliances for each cooking operation. It is one of the versatile cooking appliances capable to perform the cooking operations like air fry, whole roast, air roast, bake, broil, dehydrate, toast, pizza, bagel and reheat.

- Large cooking capacity

The Ninja Foodi XL countertop oven comes with an extra-large cooking capacity. It has 4 rack positions to hold your food while cooking it gives 2 level even cooking results. The Ninja foodi holds 5 lb of chicken, 12 lb of turkey, 9 bread slices, or two 12 inch size pizzas.

- Advanced Cooking Appliance

The Ninja Foodi XL is one of the advanced cooking appliances that cook your food 30 % faster compared to another countertop oven. It used a true surround convection technique and boost 10x convection power to cook your food faster and gives you crispy and juicy cooking results. The 360 hole roast cooking technique helps to cook your chicken evenly from all the sides. You never need to rotate or flip your food pan during the cooking process.

- Saves your cooking time

The Ninja Foodi oven is equipped with a high-velocity convection fan situated at the center backside of the oven rack. It is capable to distribute the superheated air using true surround airflow. The convection fan is a unique design and capable to blow top-bottom hot airflow to give you even cooking results.

Cleaning and Maintenance

After each use, it is recommended that always clean your Ninja Foodi XL pro-air oven thoroughly. The following steps guide and help you to clean your oven easily.

1. Before starting the cleaning process unplug the oven from the power supply and allow it to cool down.
2. Remove all the accessories like air fryer basket, crumb tray, wire rack, sheet pan, and roast tray. Use a non-abrasive brush to clean the air fryer basket. The wire rack and air fryer basket are dishwasher safe but do not clean the sheet pan, roast tray, and crumb tray into the dishwasher.
3. Clean the oven interior and glass door with the help of soapy water and a soft damp cloth. Avoid using a scrubbing brush, abrasive cleaners, and harsh chemicals as it may damage the oven interior.
4. To remove the grease and tough stains over the roast tray and sheet pan, soak it overnight in soapy water solution.
5. After cleaning all the parts dry it thoroughly before placing it in their right position.
6. Now your oven is ready for next use.

FAQs

- Why the oven is not turning on?

Check the power cord is plugged into an outlet properly. Try to plug the wiry into another socket and press the power button.

- Can I reset my unit at its default settings?

Your oven is a smart device that will remember the last used settings even you unplugged your oven. To rest default settings you need to press 2 level and light button simultaneously for 5 seconds.

- Why steam comes out from the oven?

This is a normal process that happens due to high moisture food. It releases steam while the cooking process.

- Why does the fan sound come even though the power is off?

This is a normal process. The cooling fan continuously runs even the unit is turned off.

The cooling fan automatically stops when the unit temperature goes down under 95°F.

- Does the food need to rearrange while cooking?

The true surround convection technology produces powerful airflow around the food with the help of a powerful convection fan. It gives you fast crispy and even cooking results without flipping or shaking the food tray.

- How much food I have cooked in the Oven?

Due to its large capacity, you can cook a whole family food in this oven. It has a capacity to cook 5 lb of chicken, 12 lb of turkey, a sheet pan of vegetables, two 12 inch size pizzas, and more.

- How to clean sheet pan?

To remove the tough stuck food from the sheet pan, you need to soak the sheet pan. You can also use parchment paper or aluminium foil for easy cleaning.

Chapter 2: Breakfast

Mushroom Zucchini Frittata

Preparation Time: 10 minutes
Cooking Time: 20 minutes
Serve: 2

Ingredients:

- 4 eggs
- 1 cup zucchini, chopped
- 1 cup cheddar cheese
- 1/2 cup onion, chopped
- 2 tbsp milk
- 1 tbsp olive oil
- 1 cup mushrooms, sliced
- 1 cup bell peppers, chopped
- Pepper
- Salt

Directions:

1. Heat oil in a pan over medium heat.
2. Add onion, bell peppers, zucchini, and mushrooms, and sauté for 5 minutes.
3. Remove pan from heat and set aside to cool.
4. In a bowl, whisk eggs with milk, pepper, and salt.
5. Add sautéed vegetables and cheese and stir well.
6. Pour egg mixture into the greased baking dish.
7. Place the wire rack on LEVEL 2.
8. Select bake mode set the temperature to 350 F, and set time to 20 minutes. Press start to begin preheating.
9. Once the oven is preheated, place the baking dish on a wire rack and close the oven door to start cooking.
10. Cook for 20 minutes.
11. Serve and enjoy.

Nutritional Value (Amount per Serving):

- Calories 566
- Fat 46 g
- Carbohydrates 11 g
- Sugar 6 g
- Protein 32 g
- Cholesterol 112 mg

Feta Spinach Frittata

Preparation Time: 10 minutes
Cooking Time: 30 minutes
Serve: 2

Ingredients:

- 6 eggs
- 3 oz fresh spinach, chopped
- 2 oz scallions, chopped
- 2 tbsp olive oil
- 4 oz feta cheese, crumbled
- 5 oz mushrooms, sliced
- Pepper
- Salt

Directions:

1. In a bowl, whisk eggs, cheese, pepper, and salt.
2. Heat oil in a pan over medium heat. Add mushrooms and scallions and sauté for 10 minutes.
3. Add spinach and sauté for 2 minutes.
4. Pour egg mixture into the greased baking dish.
5. Place the wire rack on LEVEL 2.
6. Select bake mode set the temperature to 350 F and set time to 20 minutes. Press start to begin preheating.
7. Once the oven is preheated, place the baking dish on a wire rack and close the oven door to start cooking.
8. Cook for 20 minutes.
9. Serve and enjoy.

Nutritional Value (Amount per Serving):

- Calories 575
- Fat 48 g
- Carbohydrates 9 g
- Sugar 5 g
- Protein 29 g
- Cholesterol 542 mg

Breakfast Mushroom Quiche

Preparation Time: 10 minutes
Cooking Time: 40 minutes
Serve: 6

Ingredients:

- 6 eggs
- 8 oz can mushroom, sliced
- 1/3 cup parmesan cheese, shredded
- 1/2 cup water
- 1/2 cup heavy cream
- 2 cheese slices, cut into pieces
- 1/2 tsp garlic powder
- 10 oz frozen spinach, thawed & drained
- 1 cup mozzarella cheese, shredded
- Pepper
- Salt

Directions:

1. Spread mushrooms and spinach into the baking dish.
2. Arrange cheese on top of mushrooms and spinach.
3. In a bowl, whisk eggs with heavy cream, garlic powder, parmesan cheese, water, pepper, and salt.
4. Pour egg mixture over spinach and mushroom mixture. Top with mozzarella cheese.
5. Place the wire rack on LEVEL 2.
6. Select bake mode set the temperature to 350 F, and set time to 40 minutes. Press start to begin preheating.
7. Once the oven is preheated, place the baking dish on a wire rack and close the oven door to start cooking.
8. Cook for 40 minutes.
9. Serve and enjoy.

Nutritional Value (Amount per Serving):

- Calories 185
- Fat 13 g
- Carbohydrates 5 g
- Sugar 0.5 g
- Protein 13 g
- Cholesterol 193 mg

Italian Egg Muffins

Preparation Time: 10 minutes
Cooking Time: 20 minutes
Serve: 12

Ingredients:

- 8 eggs
- 1 cup spinach, diced
- 1/3 cup feta cheese, crumbled
- 1/4 cup milk
- 1/2 cup sun-dried tomatoes, sliced
- 5 basil leaves, chopped
- 1/2 onion, diced
- Pepper
- Salt

Directions:

1. Divide spinach, feta cheese, onion, and sun-dried tomatoes evenly into the muffin pan.
2. In a bowl, whisk eggs with milk, basil, pepper, and salt.
3. Pour egg mixture over vegetable mixture.
4. Place the wire rack on LEVEL 2.
5. Select bake mode set the temperature to 350 F and set time to 20 minutes. Press start to begin preheating.
6. Once the oven is preheated, place the muffin pan on a wire rack and close the oven door to start cooking.
7. Cook for 20 minutes.
8. Serve and enjoy.

Nutritional Value (Amount per Serving):

- Calories 55
- Fat 4 g
- Carbohydrates 1.3 g
- Sugar 1 g
- Protein 5 g
- Cholesterol 113 mg

Feta Zucchini Muffins

Preparation Time: 10 minutes
Cooking Time: 25 minutes
Serve: 4

Ingredients:

- 1 egg, lightly beaten
- 2 cups zucchini, shredded
- 1/4 cup onion, diced
- 1/2 cup feta cheese, crumbled
- Pepper
- Salt

Directions:

1. Add egg, shredded zucchini, cheese, onion, pepper, and salt into the bowl and mix well.
2. Pour egg mixture into the greased mini muffin pan.
3. Place the wire rack on LEVEL 2.
4. Select bake mode set the temperature to 350 F and set time to 25 minutes. Press start to begin preheating.
5. Once the oven is preheated, place the muffin pan on the wire rack and close the oven door to start cooking.
6. Cook for 25 minutes.
7. Serve and enjoy.

Nutritional Value (Amount per Serving):

- Calories 80
- Fat 5.3 g
- Carbohydrates 3.5 g
- Sugar 2.2 g
- Protein 5 g
- Cholesterol 63 mg

Healthy Baked Vegetable Quiche

Preparation Time: 10 minutes
Cooking Time: 30 minutes
Serve: 2

Ingredients:

- 2 cups liquid egg substitute
- 4 oz mozzarella cheese, shredded
- 1 bell pepper, chopped
- 1 cup mushrooms, sliced
- 1 tsp olive oil
- 1/2 tsp garlic powder
- 1/2 tsp onion powder
- 2 cups spinach, chopped
- Pepper
- Salt

Directions:

1. Heat oil in a pan over medium heat.
2. Add bell pepper and mushrooms to the pan and sauté until tender.
3. Remove pan from heat and let it cool.
4. In a bowl, mix liquid egg substitute, garlic powder, onion powder, spinach, cheese, pepper, and salt.
5. Stir in sautéed bell pepper and mushrooms.
6. Pour mixture into the greased baking dish.
7. Place the wire rack on LEVEL 2.
8. Select bake mode set the temperature to 350 F, and set time to 30 minutes. Press start to begin preheating.
9. Once the oven is preheated, place the baking dish on a wire rack and close the oven door to start cooking.
10. Cook for 30 minutes.
11. Serve and enjoy.

Nutritional Value (Amount per Serving):

- Calories 330
- Fat 10.4 g
- Carbohydrates 11.4 g
- Sugar 5.7 g
- Protein 48.9 g
- Cholesterol 33 mg

Nutritious Tuna Muffins

Preparation Time: 10 minutes
Cooking Time: 25 minutes
Serve: 8

Ingredients:

- 2 eggs, lightly beaten
- 1 can tuna, flaked
- 1 celery stalk, chopped
- 1 1/2 cups cheddar cheese, shredded
- 1/4 cup sour cream
- 1 tsp cayenne pepper
- 1/4 cup mayonnaise
- Pepper
- Salt

Directions:

1. Add all ingredients into the large bowl and mix until well combined and pour into the greased muffin pan.
2. Place the wire rack on LEVEL 2.
3. Select bake mode set the temperature to 350 F and set time to 25 minutes. Press start to begin preheating.
4. Once the oven is preheated, place the baking pan on a wire rack and close the oven door to start cooking.
5. Cook for 25 minutes.
6. Serve and enjoy.

Nutritional Value (Amount per Serving):

- Calories 186
- Fat 14 g
- Carbohydrates 2.6 g
- Sugar 0.7 g
- Protein 13 g
- Cholesterol 75 mg

Tomato Frittata

Preparation Time: 10 minutes
Cooking Time: 35 minutes
Serve: 6

Ingredients:

- 12 eggs
- 1/2 cup fresh basil, chopped
- 1 cup baby spinach, chopped
- 1/2 cup yogurt
- 1/2 cup cheddar cheese, grated
- 1 1/2 cups grape tomatoes, cut in half
- Pepper
- Salt

Directions:

1. Spray dish with cooking spray and set aside.
2. In a large bowl, whisk eggs and yogurt.
3. Layer spinach, basil, tomatoes, and cheese in a prepared baking dish.
4. Pour egg mixture over spinach mixture. Season with pepper and salt.
5. Place the wire rack on LEVEL 2.
6. Select bake mode set the temperature to 390 F, and set time to 35 minutes. Press start to begin preheating.
7. Once the oven is preheated, place the baking dish on a wire rack and close the oven door to start cooking.
8. Cook for 35 minutes.
9. Serve and enjoy.

Nutritional Value (Amount per Serving):

- Calories 185
- Fat 12.2 g
- Carbohydrates 4.2 g
- Sugar 3.4 g
- Protein 15.2 g
- Cholesterol 338 mg

Baked Omelette

Preparation Time: 10 minutes
Cooking Time: 45 minutes
Serve: 6

Ingredients:

- 8 eggs
- 1/2 cup mozzarella cheese, shredded
- 6 oz ham, diced and cooked
- 1 cup milk
- 1 cup bell pepper, chopped
- 1/2 cup onion, chopped
- Pepper
- Salt

Directions:

1. Spray baking dish with cooking spray and set aside.
2. In a large bowl, whisk eggs with milk, pepper, and salt. Add remaining ingredients and stir well.
3. Pour egg mixture into the prepared baking dish.
4. Place the wire rack on LEVEL 2.
5. Select bake mode set the temperature to 350 F, and set time to 45 minutes. Press start to begin preheating.
6. Once the oven is preheated, place the pan on a wire rack and close the oven door to start cooking.
7. Cook for 45 minutes.
8. Slice and serve.

Nutritional Value (Amount per Serving):

- Calories 200
- Fat 12.3 g
- Carbohydrates 6.1 g
- Sugar 3.7 g
- Protein 16.1 g
- Cholesterol 248 mg

Sausage Veggie Egg Bake

Preparation Time: 10 minutes
Cooking Time: 35 minutes
Serve: 4

Ingredients:

- 10 eggs
- 1 lb sausage, cut into 1/2-inch pieces
- 1 tsp garlic powder
- 1/2 cup milk
- 1 cup spinach, diced
- 1 cup onion, diced
- 1 cup pepper, diced
- Pepper
- Salt

Directions:

1. Spray baking dish with cooking spray and set aside.
2. In a bowl, whisk eggs with milk and spices.
3. Add veggie and sausage and stir well.
4. Pour egg mixture into the prepared baking dish.
5. Place the wire rack on LEVEL 2.
6. Select bake mode set the temperature to 390 F and set time to 35 minutes. Press start to begin preheating.
7. Once the oven is preheated, place the baking dish on a wire rack and close the oven door to start cooking.
8. Cook for 35 minutes.
9. Slice and serve.

Nutritional Value (Amount per Serving):

- Calories 655
- Fat 50.6 g
- Carbohydrates 12.6 g
- Sugar 3.3 g
- Protein 38.3 g
- Cholesterol 504 mg

Cheesy Baked Ham Omelette

Preparation Time: 10 minutes
Cooking Time: 25 minutes
Serve: 6

Ingredients:

- 8 eggs
- 1 cup mozzarella cheese, shredded
- 1/3 cup milk
- 1 cup ham, chopped
- Pepper
- Salt

Directions:

1. Spray a 9*9-inch baking dish with cooking spray and set aside.
2. In a large bowl, whisk eggs with milk, pepper, and salt. Stir in ham and cheese.
3. Pour egg mixture into the prepared baking dish.
4. Place the wire rack on LEVEL 2.
5. Select bake mode set the temperature to 390 F and set time to 25 minutes. Press start to begin preheating.
6. Once the oven is preheated, place the baking dish on a wire rack and close the oven door to start cooking.
7. Cook for 25 minutes.
8. Slice and serve.

Nutritional Value (Amount per Serving):

- Calories 205
- Fat 14.3 g
- Carbohydrates 2.2 g
- Sugar 1.2 g
- Protein 16.3 g
- Cholesterol 252 mg

Healthy Berry Oatmeal

Preparation Time: 10 minutes
Cooking Time: 20 minutes
Serve: 4

Ingredients:

- 1 egg
- 2 cups Old fashioned oats
- 1 cup blueberries
- 1/2 cup blackberries
- 1/2 cup strawberries, sliced
- 1/4 cup maple syrup
- 1 1/2 cups milk
- 1 1/2 tsp baking powder
- 1/2 tsp salt

Directions:

1. In a bowl, mix together oats, salt, and baking powder.
2. Add vanilla, egg, maple syrup, and milk and stir well.
3. Add berries and stir well.
4. Pour mixture into the greased baking dish.
5. Place the wire rack on LEVEL 2.
6. Select bake mode set the temperature to 375 F, and set time to 20 minutes. Press start to begin preheating.
7. Once the oven is preheated, place the baking dish on a wire rack and close the oven door to start cooking.
8. Cook for 20 minutes.

Nutritional Value (Amount per Serving):

- Calories 461
- Fat 8.4 g
- Carbohydrates 80 g
- Sugar 23 g
- Protein 15 g
- Cholesterol 48 mg

Kale Zucchini Bake

Preparation Time: 10 minutes
Cooking Time: 30 minutes
Serve: 4

Ingredients:

- 6 eggs
- 1 cup kale, chopped
- 1 onion, chopped
- 1 cup zucchini, shredded
- 1/2 cup milk
- 1/2 tsp dill
- 1/2 tsp oregano
- 1/2 tsp basil
- 1/2 tsp baking powder
- 1/2 cup almond flour
- 1 cup cheddar cheese, shredded
- 1/4 tsp salt

Directions:

1. Grease 9*9-inch baking dish and set aside.
2. In a large bowl, whisk eggs with milk.
3. Add remaining ingredients and stir until well combined.
4. Pour egg mixture into the prepared baking dish.
5. Place the wire rack on LEVEL 2.
6. Select bake mode set the temperature to 375 F, and set time to 30 minutes. Press start to begin preheating.
7. Once the oven is preheated, place the pan on a wire rack and close the oven door to start cooking.
8. Cook for 30 minutes.
9. Serve and enjoy.

Nutritional Value (Amount per Serving):

- Calories 329
- Fat 23 g
- Carbohydrates 11 g
- Sugar 4 g
- Protein 20 g
- Cholesterol 278 mg

Mixed Veggie Muffins

Preparation Time: 10 minutes
Cooking Time: 22 minutes
Serve: 12

Ingredients:

- 12 eggs
- 1/4 cup parmesan cheese, grated
- 3 cups mixed vegetables, chopped
- 1/4 cup milk
- 1 tsp olive oil
- 1 cup cheddar cheese, shredded
- 3 tbsp onion, minced
- 1/2 tsp mustard powder
- 1/2 tsp pepper
- 1/2 tsp salt

Directions:

1. Spray muffin pan with cooking spray and set aside.
2. Heat oil in a pan over medium heat.
3. Add mixed vegetables and sauté until tender.
4. Remove pan from heat and let it cool.
5. In a bowl, whisk eggs, seasonings, and milk.
6. Add sautéed vegetables, onion, and cheeses and whisk well.
7. Pour egg mixture into the prepared muffin pan.
8. Place the wire rack on LEVEL 2.
9. Select bake mode set the temperature to 350 F and set time to 22 minutes. Press start to begin preheating.
10. Once the oven is preheated, place the muffin pan on the wire rack and close the oven door to start cooking.
11. Cook for 22 minutes.
12. Serve and enjoy.

Nutritional Value (Amount per Serving):

- Calories 181
- Fat 11 g
- Carbohydrates 5 g
- Sugar 0.7 g
- Protein 13 g
- Cholesterol 184 mg

Cinnamon Oatmeal Cake

Preparation Time: 10 minutes
Cooking Time: 25 minutes
Serve: 8

Ingredients:

- 2 eggs
- 1 cup oats
- 1 apple, peeled & chopped
- 1 tsp cinnamon
- 1 tsp vanilla
- 3 tbsp honey
- 1 tbsp butter
- 3 tbsp yogurt
- 1/2 tsp baking powder
- 1/2 tsp baking soda

Directions:

1. Add 3/4 cup oats and remaining ingredients into the blender and blend until smooth.
2. Add remaining oats and mix well.
3. Pour batter into the parchment-lined baking pan.
4. Place the wire rack on LEVEL 2.
5. Select bake mode set the temperature to 350 F, and set time to 25 minutes. Press start to begin preheating.
6. Once the oven is preheated, place the baking pan on a wire rack and close the oven door to start cooking.
7. Cook for 25 minutes.
8. Slice and serve.

Nutritional Value (Amount per Serving):

- Calories 112
- Fat 3.3 g
- Carbohydrates 18 g
- Sugar 10 g
- Protein 3.2 g
- Cholesterol 45 mg

Chapter 3: Poultry

Juicy Turkey Breast

Preparation Time: 10 minutes
Cooking Time: 60 minutes
Serve: 10

Ingredients:

- 4 lbs turkey breast, ribs removed
- 1 tbsp olive oil
- 1/2 tbsp poultry seasoning
- 2 tsp kosher salt

Directions:

1. Brush turkey breast with oil and rub with seasoning.
2. Place turkey breast into the air fryer basket.
3. Place the wire rack on LEVEL 2.
4. Select air fry mode set the temperature to 350 F and set time to 60 minutes. Press start to begin preheating.
5. Once the oven is preheated, place the air fry basket on the wire rack and close the oven door to start cooking.
6. Cook for 60 minutes. Turn turkey breast after 20 minutes.
7. Slice and serve.

Nutritional Value (Amount per Serving):

- Calories 200
- Fat 4.4 g
- Carbohydrates 7.8 g
- Sugar 6.4 g
- Protein 31 g
- Cholesterol 78 mg

Delicious Turkey Patties

Preparation Time: 10 minutes
Cooking Time: 14 minutes
Serve: 2

Ingredients:

- 8 oz ground turkey breast
- 1 1/2 tbsp olive oil
- 2 garlic cloves, minced
- 1/2 tsp red pepper, crushed
- 2 tsp fresh oregano, chopped
- 1/4 tsp salt

Directions:

1. Add ground turkey and remaining ingredients into the bowl and mix until well combined.
2. Make patties from the mixture and place it into the air fryer basket.
3. Place the wire rack on LEVEL 2.
4. Select air fry mode set the temperature to 360 F and set time to 14 minutes. Press start to begin preheating.
5. Once the oven is preheated, place the air fry basket on the wire rack and close the oven door to start cooking.
6. Cook for 14 minutes.
7. Serve and enjoy.

Nutritional Value (Amount per Serving):

- Calories 325
- Fat 19.2 g
- Carbohydrates 4.2 g
- Sugar 1.6 g
- Protein 33.2 g
- Cholesterol 84 mg

Chicken Zucchini Patties

Preparation Time: 10 minutes
Cooking Time: 10 minutes
Serve: 5

Ingredients:

- 1 lb ground chicken
- 1/4 cup almond flour
- 6 oz zucchini, grated
- 1 tbsp onion, grated
- 1 garlic clove, grated
- Pepper
- Salt

Directions:

1. Add ground chicken and remaining ingredients into the bowl and mix until well combined.
2. Make patties from the mixture and place it into the air fryer basket.
3. Place the wire rack on LEVEL 2.
4. Select air fry mode set the temperature to 370 F and set time to 10 minutes. Press start to begin preheating.
5. Once the oven is preheated, place the air fry basket on the wire rack and close the oven door to start cooking.
6. Cook for 10 minutes.
7. Serve and enjoy.

Nutritional Value (Amount per Serving):

- Calories 190
- Fat 10.7 g
- Carbohydrates 1.8 g
- Sugar 0.7 g
- Protein 25.6 g
- Cholesterol 93 mg

Rosemary Garlic Turkey Breast

Preparation Time: 10 minutes
Cooking Time: 40 minutes
Serve: 6

Ingredients:

- 2 lbs turkey breast
- 3 garlic cloves, minced
- 4 tbsp butter, melted
- 1 tsp fresh rosemary, chopped
- 1 tsp fresh thyme, chopped
- Pepper
- Salt

Directions:

1. Season turkey breast with pepper and salt.
2. In a small bowl, mix butter, rosemary, thyme, and garlic.
3. Brush butter mixture all over turkey breast.
4. Place turkey breast into the air fryer basket.
5. Place the wire rack on LEVEL 2.
6. Select air fry mode set the temperature to 375 F and set time to 40 minutes. Press start to begin preheating.
7. Once the oven is preheated, place the air fry basket on the wire rack and close the oven door to start cooking.
8. Cook for 40 minutes.
9. Slice and serve.

Nutritional Value (Amount per Serving):

- Calories 230
- Fat 10.2 g
- Carbohydrates 7.1 g
- Sugar 5.3 g
- Protein 26 g
- Cholesterol 85 mg

Herb Turkey Breast

Preparation Time: 10 minutes
Cooking Time: 60 minutes
Serve: 8

Ingredients:

- 2 1/2 lbs turkey breast, bone-in & skin-on
- 1 tbsp butter, softened
- 1/4 tsp pepper
- 1/2 tsp fresh sage, chopped
- 1/2 tsp fresh thyme, chopped
- 1 tsp salt

Directions:

1. In a small bowl, mix butter, sage, thyme, pepper, and salt.
2. Rub the butter mixture all over the turkey breast.
3. Place turkey breast into the air fryer basket.
4. Place the wire rack on LEVEL 2.
5. Select air fry mode set the temperature to 325 F and set time to 60 minutes. Press start to begin preheating.
6. Once the oven is preheated, place the air fry basket on the wire rack and close the oven door to start cooking.
7. Cook for 60 minutes. Turn turkey breast halfway through.
8. Slice and serve.

Nutritional Value (Amount per Serving):

- Calories 160
- Fat 3.8 g
- Carbohydrates 6.1 g
- Sugar 5 g
- Protein 24.2 g
- Cholesterol 65 mg

Adobo Chicken

Preparation Time: 10 minutes
Cooking Time: 20 minutes
Serve: 4

Ingredients:

- 4 chicken thighs
- 2 tbsp Adobo seasoning
- 1 tbsp olive oil

Directions:

1. Rub chicken thighs with oil and adobo seasoning.
2. Place chicken thighs into the air fryer basket.
3. Place the wire rack on LEVEL 2.
4. Select air fry mode set the temperature to 350 F and set time to 20 minutes. Press start to begin preheating.
5. Once the oven is preheated, place the air fry basket on the wire rack and close the oven door to start cooking.
6. Cook for 20 minutes. Turn chicken halfway through.
7. Serve and enjoy.

Nutritional Value (Amount per Serving):

- Calories 305
- Fat 14.3 g
- Carbohydrates 0 g
- Sugar 0 g
- Protein 42.2 g
- Cholesterol 130 mg

Crispy Chicken Wings

Preparation Time: 10 minutes
Cooking Time: 20 minutes
Serve: 4

Ingredients:

- 2 lbs chicken wings
- 1 tsp smoked paprika
- 2 tsp garlic powder
- 2 tsp onion powder
- 1/2 tbsp thyme
- 1/2 tsp cayenne pepper
- 1 tsp white pepper

Directions:

1. In a small bowl, mix cayenne pepper, white pepper, paprika, garlic powder, onion powder, and thyme.
2. Rub chicken wings with spice mixture and place into the air fryer basket.
3. Place the wire rack on LEVEL 2.
4. Select air fry mode set the temperature to 400 F and set time to 20 minutes. Press start to begin preheating.
5. Once the oven is preheated, place the air fry basket on the wire rack and close the oven door to start cooking.
6. Cook for 20 minutes. Turn chicken wings halfway through.
7. Serve and enjoy.

Nutritional Value (Amount per Serving):

- Calories 445
- Fat 17 g
- Carbohydrates 3 g
- Sugar 0.9 g
- Protein 66.2 g
- Cholesterol 202 mg

Ranch Chicken Wings

Preparation Time: 10 minutes
Cooking Time: 30 minutes
Serve: 4

Ingredients:

- 2 lbs chicken wings
- 1 tsp olive oil
- 1 tsp ranch seasoning
- 1 1/2 tsp taco seasoning

Directions:

1. In a bowl, add chicken wings, ranch seasoning, taco seasoning, and oil and toss well to coat.
2. Place chicken wings into the air fryer basket.
3. Place the wire rack on LEVEL 2.
4. Select air fry mode set the temperature to 400 F and set time to 30 minutes. Press start to begin preheating.
5. Once the oven is preheated, place the air fry basket on the wire rack and close the oven door to start cooking.
6. Cook for 30 minutes. Turn chicken wings halfway through.
7. Serve and enjoy.

Nutritional Value (Amount per Serving):

- Calories 445
- Fat 18 g
- Carbohydrates 0 g
- Sugar 0 g
- Protein 65.6 g
- Cholesterol 202 mg

Turkey Burger Patties

Preparation Time: 10 minutes
Cooking Time: 20 minutes
Serve: 4

Ingredients:

- 1 lb ground turkey
- 1 tbsp olive oil
- 1 tbsp garlic, minced
- 4 oz feta cheese, crumbled
- 1 1/2 cups fresh spinach, chopped
- 1 tsp Italian seasoning
- Pepper
- Salt

Directions:

1. Add ground turkey and remaining ingredients into the bowl and mix until well combined.
2. Make patties from turkey mixture and place it into the air fryer basket.
3. Place the wire rack on LEVEL 2.
4. Select air fry mode set the temperature to 350 F and set time to 20 minutes. Press start to begin preheating.
5. Once the oven is preheated, place the air fry basket on the wire rack and close the oven door to start cooking.
6. Cook for 20 minutes.
7. Serve and enjoy.

Nutritional Value (Amount per Serving):

- Calories 335
- Fat 22.4 g
- Carbohydrates 2.4 g
- Sugar 1.3 g
- Protein 35.5 g
- Cholesterol 142 mg

Spicy Chicken Wings

Preparation Time: 10 minutes
Cooking Time: 30 minutes
Serve: 4

Ingredients:

- 2 lbs chicken wings
- 1/4 tsp smoked paprika
- 2 tsp garlic powder
- 4 tsp chili powder
- 3 tbsp olive oil
- Pepper
- Salt

Directions:

1. Add chicken wings and remaining ingredients into the zip-lock bag and shake well to coat.
2. Place the wire rack on LEVEL 2.
3. Select air fry mode set the temperature to 380 F and set time to 30 minutes. Press start to begin preheating.
4. Once the oven is preheated, place the air fry basket on the wire rack and close the oven door to start cooking.
5. Cook for 30 minutes. Turn halfway through.
6. Serve and enjoy.

Nutritional Value (Amount per Serving):

- Calories 535
- Fat 27.8 g
- Carbohydrates 2.5 g
- Sugar 0.5 g
- Protein 66.2 g
- Cholesterol 202 mg

Baked Chicken Thighs

Preparation Time: 10 minutes
Cooking Time: 35 minutes
Serve: 4

Ingredients:

- 4 chicken thighs
- 2 tbsp olive oil
- 2 tsp poultry seasoning
- Pepper
- Salt

Directions:

1. Brush chicken with oil and rub with poultry seasoning, pepper, and salt.
2. Arrange chicken on a sheet pan.
3. Place the wire rack on LEVEL 2.
4. Select bake mode set the temperature to 390 F and set time to 35 minutes. Press start to begin preheating.
5. Once the oven is preheated, place a sheet pan on a wire rack and close the oven door to start cooking.
6. Cook for 35 minutes.
7. Serve and enjoy.

Nutritional Value (Amount per Serving):

- Calories 320
- Fat 15.5 g
- Carbohydrates 0.3 g
- Sugar 0 g
- Protein 42.3 g
- Cholesterol 130 mg

BBQ Chicken Wings

Preparation Time: 10 minutes
Cooking Time: 55 minutes
Serve: 8

Ingredients:

- 32 chicken wings
- 1/4 cup olive oil
- 1 1/2 cups BBQ sauce
- Pepper
- Salt

Directions:

1. In a bowl, toss chicken wings with olive oil, pepper, and salt.
2. Arrange chicken wings on a sheet pan.
3. Place the wire rack on LEVEL 2.
4. Select bake mode set the temperature to 375 F and set time to 50 minutes. Press start to begin preheating.
5. Once the oven is preheated, place the pan on a wire rack and close the oven door to start cooking.
6. Cook for 50 minutes. Toss chicken wings with BBQ sauce and bake for 5 minutes more.
7. Serve and enjoy.

Nutritional Value (Amount per Serving):

- Calories 175
- Fat 8.3 g
- Carbohydrates 17 g
- Sugar 12.2 g
- Protein 7.4 g
- Cholesterol 23 mg

Honey Mustard Chicken

Preparation Time: 10 minutes
Cooking Time: 40 minutes
Serve: 6

Ingredients:

- 6 chicken thighs, bone-in & skin-on
- 1/2 cup honey
- 1/4 cup mustard
- Pepper
- Salt

Directions:

1. Season chicken with pepper and salt and place into the baking dish.
2. Mix mustard and honey and pour over chicken.
3. Place the wire rack on LEVEL 2.
4. Select bake mode set the temperature to 350 F and set time to 30 minutes. Press start to begin preheating.
5. Once the oven is preheated, place the baking dish on a wire rack and close the oven door to start cooking.
6. Cook for 30 minutes. Spoon honey mustard mixture over chicken and bake chicken 10 minutes more.
7. Serve and enjoy.

Nutritional Value (Amount per Serving):

- Calories 120
- Fat 1.4 g
- Carbohydrates 24 g
- Sugar 23.3 g
- Protein 4.5 g
- Cholesterol 12 mg

Chicken Thighs & Potatoes

Preparation Time: 10 minutes
Cooking Time: 60 minutes
Serve: 5

Ingredients:

- 5 chicken thighs
- 1 tbsp fresh rosemary, chopped
- 1 tsp dried oregano
- 2 lbs potatoes, cut into chunks
- 5 garlic cloves, minced
- 1 lemon juice
- 1/2 cup olive oil
- Pepper
- Salt

Directions:

1. In a large bowl, add chicken and remaining ingredients and mix well.
2. Place chicken in the baking dish and spread potatoes around the chicken.
3. Place the wire rack on LEVEL 2.
4. Select bake mode set the temperature to 375 F and set time to 60 minutes. Press start to begin preheating.
5. Once the oven is preheated, place the baking dish on a wire rack and close the oven door to start cooking.
6. Cook for 60 minutes.
7. Serve and enjoy.

Nutritional Value (Amount per Serving):

- Calories 335
- Fat 21.6 g
- Carbohydrates 30.1 g
- Sugar 2.3 g
- Protein 7.3 g
- Cholesterol 12 mg

Crispy Parmesan Chicken

Preparation Time: 10 minutes
Cooking Time: 35 minutes
Serve: 4

Ingredients:

- 4 chicken breasts
- 1/4 cup olive oil
- 1 cup breadcrumbs
- 1 cup parmesan cheese, shredded
- 1/4 tsp garlic powder
- 1/4 tsp Italian seasoning
- Pepper
- Salt

Directions:

1. Season chicken with pepper and salt and brush with olive oil.
2. In a shallow dish, mix parmesan cheese, garlic powder, Italian seasoning, and breadcrumbs.
3. Coat chicken with parmesan and breadcrumb mixture and place in the baking dish.
4. Place the wire rack on LEVEL 2.
5. Select bake mode set the temperature to 350 F and set time to 35 minutes. Press start to begin preheating.
6. Once the oven is preheated, place the baking dish on a wire rack and close the oven door to start cooking.
7. Cook for 35 minutes.
8. Serve and enjoy.

Nutritional Value (Amount per Serving):

- Calories 565
- Fat 30 g
- Carbohydrates 20.3 g
- Sugar 1.7 g
- Protein 53.1 g
- Cholesterol 146 mg

Chapter 4: Beef, Pork & Lamb

Meatballs

Preparation Time: 10 minutes
Cooking Time: 20 minutes
Serve: 4

Ingredients:

- 1/2 lb ground beef
- 1/2 lb Italian sausage
- 1/2 tsp black pepper
- 1/2 tsp garlic powder
- 1/2 tsp onion powder
- 1/2 cup cheddar cheese, shredded

Directions:

1. Add all ingredients into the bowl and mix until well combined.
2. Make balls from the mixture and place it in the air fryer basket.
3. Place the wire rack on LEVEL 2.
4. Select air fry mode set the temperature to 370 F and set time to 20 minutes. Press start to begin preheating.
5. Once the oven is preheated, place the air fry basket on the wire rack and close the oven door to start cooking.
6. Cook for 20 minutes.
7. Serve and enjoy.

Nutritional Value (Amount per Serving):

- Calories 355
- Fat 24.3 g
- Carbohydrates 0.8 g
- Sugar 0.3 g
- Protein 31.9 g
- Cholesterol 95 mg

Crispy Crusted Pork Chops

Preparation Time: 10 minutes
Cooking Time: 13 minutes
Serve: 4

Ingredients:

- 6 pork chops, boneless
- 1 1/2 cup breadcrumbs
- 2 egg, lightly beaten
- 1/4 cup flour
- 1/4 tsp pepper
- 1/4 tsp salt

Directions:

1. Add eggs, breadcrumbs, and flour in three separate shallow dishes.
2. Season pork chops with pepper and salt.
3. Coat pork chops with flour then dip in eggs and coat with breadcrumbs.
4. Place pork chops in the air fryer basket.
5. Place the wire rack on LEVEL 2.
6. Select air fry mode set the temperature to 350 F and set time to 13 minutes. Press start to begin preheating.
7. Once the oven is preheated, place the air fry basket on the wire rack and close the oven door to start cooking.
8. Cook for 13 minutes.
9. Serve and enjoy.

Nutritional Value (Amount per Serving):

- Calories 610
- Fat 37.4 g
- Carbohydrates 31.7 g
- Sugar 0.2 g
- Protein 35.1 g
- Cholesterol 185 mg

Asian Lamb

Preparation Time: 10 minutes
Cooking Time: 10 minutes
Serve: 4

Ingredients:

- 1 lb lamb, cut into 1/2-inch pieces
- 2 tbsp canola oil
- 1/4 tsp sugar
- 1 1/2 red chili peppers, chopped
- 1 tbsp garlic, minced
- 1 tbsp soy sauce
- 1/2 tsp cayenne
- 1/2 tbsp cumin powder
- 2 tbsp green onion, chopped
- 1 tsp salt

Directions:

1. In a bowl, mix lamb, cumin powder, cayenne, sugar, red chili peppers, garlic, soy sauce, oil, and salt.
2. Place marinated lamb pieces into the air fryer basket
3. Place the wire rack on LEVEL 2.
4. Select air fry mode set the temperature to 360 F and set time to 10 minutes. Press start to begin preheating.
5. Once the oven is preheated, place the air fry basket on the wire rack and close the oven door to start cooking.
6. Cook for 10 minutes.
7. Garnish with green onion and serve.

Nutritional Value (Amount per Serving):

- Calories 285
- Fat 15.7 g
- Carbohydrates 2.3 g
- Sugar 0.5 g
- Protein 32.5 g
- Cholesterol 102 mg

Meatballs

Preparation Time: 10 minutes
Cooking Time: 8 minutes
Serve: 5

Ingredients:

- 5 oz ground beef
- 1/2 tbsp lemon zest, grated
- 1 tbsp fresh oregano, chopped
- 2 oz feta cheese, crumbled
- 2 tbsp almond flour
- Pepper
- Salt

Directions:

1. Add all ingredients into the bowl and mix until well combined.
2. Make balls from meat mixture and place meatballs into the air fryer basket.
3. Place the wire rack on LEVEL 2.
4. Select air fry mode set the temperature to 400 F and set time to 8 minutes. Press start to begin preheating.
5. Once the oven is preheated, place the air fry basket on the wire rack and close the oven door to start cooking.
6. Cook for 8 minutes.
7. Serve and enjoy.

Nutritional Value (Amount per Serving):

- Calories 106
- Fat 5.8 g
- Carbohydrates 1.8 g
- Sugar 0.6 g
- Protein 11.4 g
- Cholesterol 37 mg

Flavorful Marinated Steak

Preparation Time: 5 minutes
Cooking Time: 8 minutes
Serve: 2

Ingredients:

- 12 oz steaks
- 1 tbsp soy sauce
- 1/2 tbsp cocoa powder
- 1 tbsp Montreal steak seasoning
- Pepper
- Salt

Directions:

1. Add steak, soy sauce, and seasonings into the large zip-lock bag.
2. Shake well and place it in the refrigerator overnight.
3. Place marinated steaks into the air fryer basket.
4. Place the wire rack on LEVEL 2.
5. Select air fry mode set the temperature to 350 F and set time to 8 minutes. Press start to begin preheating.
6. Once the oven is preheated, place the air fry basket on the wire rack and close the oven door to start cooking.
7. Cook for 8 minutes.
8. Serve and enjoy.

Nutritional Value (Amount per Serving):

- Calories 355
- Fat 9 g
- Carbohydrates 1.4 g
- Sugar 0.2 g
- Protein 63 g
- Cholesterol 3 mg

Crispy Parmesan Pork Chops

Preparation Time: 10 minutes
Cooking Time: 12 minutes
Serve: 6

Ingredients:

- 1 1/2 lbs pork chops, boneless
- 1/3 cup almond flour
- 1 tsp paprika
- 1 tsp Creole seasoning
- 1 tsp garlic powder
- 1/4 cup parmesan cheese, grated

Directions:

1. Add all ingredients except pork chops into the zip-lock bag.
2. Add pork chops into the bag. Seal bag and shake well.
3. Remove pork chops from the zip-lock bag and place it into the air fryer basket.
4. Place the wire rack on LEVEL 2.
5. Select air fry mode set the temperature to 400 F and set time to 12 minutes. Press start to begin preheating.
6. Once the oven is preheated, place the air fry basket on the wire rack and close the oven door to start cooking.
7. Cook for 12 minutes.
8. Serve and enjoy.

Nutritional Value (Amount per Serving):

- Calories 400
- Fat 30.5 g
- Carbohydrates 0.9 g
- Sugar 0.2 g
- Protein 27.9 g
- Cholesterol 11 mg

Juicy Pork Chops

Preparation Time: 5 minutes
Cooking Time: 16 minutes
Serve: 4

Ingredients:

- 4 pork chops, boneless
- 2 tsp olive oil
- 1/2 tsp celery seed
- 1/2 tsp parsley
- 1/2 tsp onion powder
- 1/2 tsp garlic powder
- 1/4 tsp sugar
- 1/2 tsp salt

Directions:

1. In a small bowl, mix sugar, garlic powder, onion powder, parsley, celery seed, and salt.
2. Rub oil and seasoning on the pork chops.
3. Place pork chops in the air fryer basket.
4. Place the wire rack on LEVEL 2.
5. Select bake mode set the temperature to 350 F and set time to 16 minutes. Press start to begin preheating.
6. Once the oven is preheated, place the pan on a wire rack and close the oven door to start cooking.
7. Cook for 16 minutes.
8. Serve and enjoy.

Nutritional Value (Amount per Serving):

- Calories 281s
- Fat 22.3 g
- Carbohydrates 0.9 g
- Sugar 0.5 g
- Protein 18.1 g
- Cholesterol 69 mg

Jalapeno Meatballs

Preparation Time: 10 minutes
Cooking Time: 35 minutes
Serve: 4

Ingredients:

- 1 lb ground beef
- 1/3 cup milk
- 1/2 cup cheddar cheese, shredded
- 3/4 cup breadcrumbs
- 2 jalapenos, minced
- 4 oz cream cheese
- 1 tsp dried basil
- 2 tbsp Worcestershire sauce
- 1/2 onion, minced
- 1 tsp salt

Directions:

1. Add all ingredients into the bowl and mix until well combined.
2. Make balls from the meat mixture and place onto the parchment-lined sheet pan.
3. Place the wire rack on LEVEL 2.
4. Select bake mode set the temperature to 400 F and set time to 35 minutes. Press start to begin preheating.
5. Once the oven is preheated, place a sheet pan on a wire rack and close the oven door to start cooking.
6. Cook for 35 minutes.
7. Serve and enjoy.

Nutritional Value (Amount per Serving):

- Calories 475
- Fat 23.2 g
- Carbohydrates 19.7 g
- Sugar 4.6 g
- Protein 43.7 g
- Cholesterol 149 mg

Tender Pork Chops

Preparation Time: 10 minutes
Cooking Time: 15 minutes
Serve: 4

Ingredients:

- 4 pork chops, boneless
- 1/4 cup olive oil
- 1 tsp pepper
- 1 tsp onion powder
- 1 tsp smoked paprika
- 2 tsp salt

Directions:

1. Brush pork chops with oil and season with onion powder, paprika, pepper, and salt.
2. Place pork chops on a sheet pan.
3. Place the wire rack on LEVEL 2.
4. Select bake mode set the temperature to 400 F and set time to 15 minutes. Press start to begin preheating.
5. Once the oven is preheated, place a sheet pan on a wire rack and close the oven door to start cooking.
6. Cook for 15 minutes.
7. Serve and enjoy.

Nutritional Value (Amount per Serving):

- Calories 370
- Fat 32.6 g
- Carbohydrates 1.1 g
- Sugar 0.3 g
- Protein 18.2 g
- Cholesterol 69 mg

Pesto Pork Chops

Preparation Time: 10 minutes
Cooking Time: 25 minutes
Serve: 6

Ingredients:

- 6 pork chops
- 1/2 cup pesto
- 2 tbsp olive oil
- Pepper
- Salt

Directions:

1. Brush pork chops with oil and season with pepper and salt.
2. Place pork chops into the baking dish.
3. Pour pesto over pork chops.
4. Place the wire rack on LEVEL 2.
5. Select bake mode set the temperature to 425 F and set time to 25 minutes. Press start to begin preheating.
6. Once the oven is preheated, place the baking dish on a wire rack and close the oven door to start cooking.
7. Cook for 25 minutes.
8. Serve and enjoy.

Nutritional Value (Amount per Serving):

- Calories 415
- Fat 33.5 g
- Carbohydrates 7.2 g
- Sugar 5.3 g
- Protein 21.3 g
- Cholesterol 74 mg

Delicious Baked Pork Ribs

Preparation Time: 10 minutes
Cooking Time: 30 minutes
Serve: 8

Ingredients:

- 2 lbs pork ribs, boneless
- 1 1/2 tbsp garlic powder
- 1 tbsp onion powder
- Pepper
- Salt

Directions:

1. Place pork ribs on sheet pan and season with onion powder, garlic powder, pepper, and salt.
2. Place the wire rack on LEVEL 2.
3. Select bake mode set the temperature to 350 F and set time to 30 minutes. Press start to begin preheating.
4. Once the oven is preheated, sheet pan on a wire rack and close the oven door to start cooking.
5. Cook for 30 minutes.
6. Serve and enjoy.

Nutritional Value (Amount per Serving):

- Calories 315
- Fat 20.1 g
- Carbohydrates 1.9 g
- Sugar 0.7 g
- Protein 30.4 g
- Cholesterol 117 mg

Beef Tips

Preparation Time: 10 minutes
Cooking Time: 20 minutes
Serve: 6

Ingredients:

- 2 lbs sirloin steak, cut into 1-inch cubes
- 1 tsp onion powder
- 1 tsp dried oregano
- 2 tbsp lemon juice
- 2 tbsp water
- 1/4 cup olive oil
- 1 cup parsley, chopped
- 1/4 tsp red chili flakes
- 1/2 tsp pepper
- 1/2 tsp dried thyme
- 1 tsp garlic, minced
- 1/2 tsp salt

Directions:

1. Add all ingredients into the zip-lock bag, seal bag shakes well and place in the refrigerator for 1 hour.
2. Place marinated steak cubes onto the sheet pan.
3. Place the wire rack on LEVEL 2.
4. Select bake mode set the temperature to 400 F and set time to 20 minutes. Press start to begin preheating.
5. Once the oven is preheated, place a sheet pan on a wire rack and close the oven door to start cooking.
6. Cook for 20 minutes.
7. Serve and enjoy.

Nutritional Value (Amount per Serving):

- Calories 360
- Fat 18 g
- Carbohydrates 1.6 g
- Sugar 0.4 g
- Protein 46.3 g
- Cholesterol 135 mg

Lamb Patties

Preparation Time: 10 minutes
Cooking Time: 15 minutes
Serve: 4

Ingredients:

- 1 lb ground lamb
- 1/4 cup onion, minced
- 1 tbsp garlic, minced
- 1/4 tsp cayenne pepper
- 1/2 tsp ground allspice
- 1 tsp ground cinnamon
- 1 tsp ground coriander
- 1 tsp ground cumin
- 1/4 cup fresh parsley, chopped
- 1/4 tsp pepper
- 1 tsp kosher salt

Directions:

1. Add all ingredients into the mixing bowl and mix until well combined.
2. Make patties from meat mixture and place onto the sheet pan.
3. Place the wire rack on LEVEL 2.
4. Select bake mode set the temperature to 450 F and set time to 15 minutes. Press start to begin preheating.
5. Once the oven is preheated, place a sheet pan on a wire rack and close the oven door to start cooking.
6. Cook for 15 minutes.
7. Serve and enjoy.

Nutritional Value (Amount per Serving):

- Calories 225
- Fat 8.5 g
- Carbohydrates 2.6 g
- Sugar 0.4 g
- Protein 32.3 g
- Cholesterol 102 mg

Chapter 5: Fish & Seafood

Salmon Cakes

Preparation Time: 10 minutes
Cooking Time: 20 minutes
Serve: 4

Ingredients:

- 14 oz can salmon, drained
- 2 eggs, lightly beaten
- 1/2 cup fresh parsley, chopped
- 1 tsp Dijon mustard
- 1/4 tsp pepper
- 1 tbsp garlic, minced
- 1/4 cup almond flour
- 1/2 tsp kosher salt

Directions:

1. Spray sheet pan with cooking spray.
2. Add all ingredients into the bowl and mix until well combined.
3. Make small patties from the mixture and place them on a sheet pan.
4. Place the wire rack on LEVEL 2.
5. Select bake mode set the temperature to 400 F and set time to 20 minutes. Press start to begin preheating.
6. Once the oven is preheated, place a sheet pan on a wire rack and close the oven door to start cooking.
7. Cook for 20 minutes.
8. Serve and enjoy.

Nutritional Value (Amount per Serving):

- Calories 215
- Fat 11 g
- Carbohydrates 3 g
- Sugar 0.5 g
- Protein 24.3 g
- Cholesterol 136 mg

Rosemary Basil Salmon

Preparation Time: 10 minutes
Cooking Time: 15 minutes
Serve: 4

Ingredients:

- 1 lbs salmon, cut into 4 pieces
- 1/4 tsp dried basil
- 1 tbsp olive oil
- 1/2 tbsp dried rosemary
- Pepper
- Salt

Directions:

1. Place salmon pieces into the air fryer basket.
2. In a small bowl, mix olive oil, basil, and rosemary.
3. Brush salmon with oil mixture.
4. Place the wire rack on LEVEL 2.
5. Select air fry mode set the temperature to 400 F and set time to 15 minutes. Press start to begin preheating.
6. Once the oven is preheated, place the air fry basket on the wire rack and close the oven door to start cooking.
7. Cook for 15 minutes.
8. Serve and enjoy.

Nutritional Value (Amount per Serving):

- Calories 180
- Fat 10.6 g
- Carbohydrates 0.3 g
- Sugar 0 g
- Protein 22 g
- Cholesterol 50 mg

Delicious White Fish Fillet

Preparation Time: 10 minutes
Cooking Time: 30 minutes
Serve: 1

Ingredients:

- 8 oz frozen white fish fillet
- 1 tbsp fresh parsley, chopped
- 1 1/2 tbsp olive oil
- 1 tbsp lemon juice
- 1 tbsp roasted red bell pepper, diced
- 1/2 tsp Italian seasoning

Directions:

1. Place a fish fillet on a sheet pan.
2. Drizzle oil and lemon juice over fish. Season with Italian seasoning.
3. Top with bell pepper and parsley.
4. Place the wire rack on LEVEL 2.
5. Select bake mode set the temperature to 400 F and set time to 30 minutes. Press start to begin preheating.
6. Once the oven is preheated, place a sheet pan on a wire rack and close the oven door to start cooking.
7. Cook for 30 minutes.
8. Serve and enjoy.

Nutritional Value (Amount per Serving):

- Calories 382
- Fat 22.5 g
- Carbohydrates 0.8 g
- Sugar 0.6 g
- Protein 46.5 g
- Cholesterol 2 mg

Italian Salmon

Preparation Time: 10 minutes
Cooking Time: 20 minutes
Serve: 5

Ingredients:

- 1 3/4 lbs salmon fillet
- 1 tbsp fresh dill, chopped
- 1/4 cup capers
- 1/3 cup artichoke hearts
- 1 tsp paprika
- 1/3 cup basil pesto
- 1/4 cup sun-dried tomatoes, drained
- 1/4 cup olives, pitted and chopped
- 1/4 tsp salt

Directions:

1. Arrange salmon fillet on a sheet pan and season with paprika and salt.
2. Add remaining ingredients on top of salmon.
3. Place the wire rack on LEVEL 2.
4. Select bake mode set the temperature to 400 F and set time to 20 minutes. Press start to begin preheating.
5. Once the oven is preheated, place a sheet pan on a wire rack and close the oven door to start cooking.
6. Cook for 20 minutes.
7. Serve and enjoy.

Nutritional Value (Amount per Serving):

- Calories 225
- Fat 10.7 g
- Carbohydrates 2.7 g
- Sugar 0.3 g
- Protein 31.6 g
- Cholesterol 70 mg

Dijon Salmon

Preparation Time: 10 minutes
Cooking Time: 20 minutes
Serve: 5

Ingredients:

- 1 1/2 lbs salmon
- 1/4 cup Dijon mustard
- 1 tbsp olive oil
- 1 tbsp fresh lemon juice
- 1/4 cup fresh parsley, chopped
- 1 tbsp garlic, chopped
- Pepper
- Salt

Directions:

1. Arrange salmon fillets on a sheet pan.
2. In a small bowl, mix garlic, oil, lemon juice, Dijon mustard, parsley, pepper, and salt.
3. Brush salmon top with garlic mixture.
4. Place the wire rack on LEVEL 2.
5. Select bake mode set the temperature to 375 F and set time to 20 minutes. Press start to begin preheating.
6. Once the oven is preheated, place a sheet pan on a wire rack and close the oven door to start cooking.
7. Cook for 20 minutes.
8. Serve and enjoy.

Nutritional Value (Amount per Serving):

- Calories 215
- Fat 11 g
- Carbohydrates 2 g
- Sugar 0.2 g
- Protein 27 g
- Cholesterol 60 mg

Blackened Fish Fillets

Preparation Time: 10 minutes
Cooking Time: 12 minutes
Serve: 4

Ingredients:

- 1 1/4 lbs tilapia fillets
- 2 tsp onion powder
- 2 tbsp paprika
- 2 tbsp olive oil
- 1 tsp black pepper
- 1/2 tsp garlic powder
- 1/2 tsp dried thyme
- 1/2 tsp oregano
- 1 tsp chili powder
- 1/2 tsp salt

Directions:

1. Brush fish fillets with oil and place them on a sheet pan.
2. Mix together spices and rub all over the fish fillets.
3. Place the wire rack on LEVEL 2.
4. Select bake mode set the temperature to 425 F and set time to 12 minutes. Press start to begin preheating.
5. Once the oven is preheated, place a sheet pan on a wire rack and close the oven door to start cooking.
6. Cook for 12 minutes.
7. Serve and enjoy.

Nutritional Value (Amount per Serving):

- Calories 195
- Fat 8.9 g
- Carbohydrates 4 g
- Sugar 0.9 g
- Protein 27.2 g
- Cholesterol 69 mg

Lemon Pepper Fish Fillets

Preparation Time: 10 minutes
Cooking Time: 12 minutes
Serve: 4

Ingredients:

- 4 basa fish fillets
- 2 tbsp fresh parsley, chopped
- 1/4 cup green onion, sliced
- 1/2 tsp garlic powder
- 1/4 tsp lemon pepper seasoning
- 4 tbsp fresh lemon juice
- 8 tsp olive oil
- Pepper
- Salt

Directions:

1. Place fish fillets in a baking dish.
2. Pour remaining ingredients over fish fillets.
3. Place the wire rack on LEVEL 2.
4. Select bake mode set the temperature to 425 F and set time to 12 minutes. Press start to begin preheating.
5. Once the oven is preheated, place the baking dish on a wire rack and close the oven door to start cooking.
6. Cook for 12 minutes.
7. Serve and enjoy.

Nutritional Value (Amount per Serving):

- Calories 305
- Fat 21 g
- Carbohydrates 5 g
- Sugar 3 g
- Protein 24 g
- Cholesterol 0 mg

Tasty Shrimp Fajitas

Preparation Time: 10 minutes
Cooking Time: 20 minutes
Serve: 12

Ingredients:

- 1 lb shrimp
- 2 tbsp fajita seasoning
- 1 green bell pepper, diced
- 1 red bell pepper, diced
- 1/2 cup onion, diced
- 1 tbsp olive oil

Directions:

1. Add shrimp and remaining ingredients into the bowl and toss well.
2. Add shrimp mixture into the air fryer basket.
3. Place the wire rack on LEVEL 2.
4. Select air fry mode set the temperature to 390 F and set time to 20 minutes. Press start to begin preheating.
5. Once the oven is preheated, place the air fry basket on the wire rack and close the oven door to start cooking.
6. Cook for 20 minutes.
7. Serve and enjoy.

Nutritional Value (Amount per Serving):

- Calories 60
- Fat 2 g
- Carbohydrates 2 g
- Sugar 0.7 g
- Protein 8 g
- Cholesterol 80 mg

Rosemary Garlic Shrimp

Preparation Time: 10 minutes
Cooking Time: 10 minutes
Serve: 4

Ingredients:

- 1 lb shrimp, peeled and deveined
- 2 garlic cloves, minced
- 1/2 tbsp fresh rosemary, chopped
- 1 tbsp olive oil
- Pepper
- Salt

Directions:

1. Add shrimp and remaining ingredients in a large bowl and toss well.
2. Pour shrimp mixture into the baking dish.
3. Place the wire rack on LEVEL 2.
4. Select bake mode set the temperature to 400 F and set time to 10 minutes. Press start to begin preheating.
5. Once the oven is preheated, place the baking dish on a wire rack and close the oven door to start cooking.
6. Cook for 10 minutes.
7. Serve and enjoy.

Nutritional Value (Amount per Serving):

- Calories 165
- Fat 5 g
- Carbohydrates 2 g
- Sugar 0 g
- Protein 26 g
- Cholesterol 240 mg

Air Fryer Blackened Shrimp

Preparation Time: 10 minutes
Cooking Time: 6 minutes
Serve: 4

Ingredients:

- 1 lb shrimp, peeled and deveined
- 2 tsp paprika
- 1 tsp onion powder
- 2 tbsp olive oil
- 1/4 tsp cayenne
- 1 tsp dried oregano
- 1 tsp garlic powder
- Pepper
- Salt

Directions:

1. In a bowl, toss shrimp with remaining ingredients.
2. Add shrimp into the air fryer basket.
3. Place the wire rack on LEVEL 2.
4. Select air fry mode set the temperature to 400 F and set time to 6 minutes. Press start to begin preheating.
5. Once the oven is preheated, place the air fry basket on the wire rack and close the oven door to start cooking.
6. Cook for 6 minutes.
7. Serve and enjoy.

Nutritional Value (Amount per Serving):

- Calories 206
- Fat 9 g
- Carbohydrates 3 g
- Sugar 0.5 g
- Protein 26 g
- Cholesterol 240 mg

Rosemary Basil Herb Salmon

Preparation Time: 10 minutes

Cooking Time: 15 minutes

Serve: 4

Ingredients:

- 1 lbs salmon, cut into 4 pieces
- 1/2 tbsp dried rosemary
- 1 tbsp olive oil
- 1/4 tsp dried basil
- Pepper
- Salt

Directions:

1. Place salmon into the air fryer basket.
2. Mix olive oil, basil, chives, and rosemary in a small bowl.
3. Brush salmon with oil mixture.
4. Place the wire rack on LEVEL 2.
5. Select air fry mode set the temperature to 400 F and set time to 15 minutes. Press start to begin preheating.
6. Once the oven is preheated, place the air fry basket on the wire rack and close the oven door to start cooking.
7. Cook for 15 minutes.
8. Serve and enjoy.

Nutritional Value (Amount per Serving):

- Calories 180
- Fat 10 g
- Carbohydrates 0.3 g
- Sugar 0 g
- Protein 22 g
- Cholesterol 50 mg

Old Bay Shrimp

Preparation Time: 10 minutes
Cooking Time: 6 minutes
Serve: 2

Ingredients:

- 1/2 lb shrimp, peeled and deveined
- 1/2 tsp old bay seasoning
- 1/2 tsp cayenne pepper
- 1 tbsp olive oil
- 1/4 tsp paprika
- Pinch of salt

Directions:

1. Add shrimp and remaining ingredients into the bowl and toss well.
2. Add shrimp into the air fryer basket.
3. Place the wire rack on LEVEL 2.
4. Select air fry mode set the temperature to 390 F and set time to 6 minutes. Press start to begin preheating.
5. Once the oven is preheated, place the air fry basket on the wire rack and close the oven door to start cooking.
6. Cook for 6 minutes.
7. Serve and enjoy.

Nutritional Value (Amount per Serving):

- Calories 195
- Fat 9 g
- Carbohydrates 2.1 g
- Sugar 0.1 g
- Protein 25.9 g
- Cholesterol 239 mg

Crispy Coconut Shrimp

Preparation Time: 10 minutes

Cooking Time: 8 minutes

Serve: 8

Ingredients:

- 2 eggs, lightly beaten
- 1 lb large shrimp, peeled and deveined
- 1/4 tsp garlic powder
- 1 cup flaked coconut
- 1/4 cup coconut flour

Directions:

1. In a small bowl, add coconut flour.
2. In a shallow bowl, add eggs.
3. In a separate shallow bowl, add flaked coconut and garlic powder.
4. Coat shrimp with coconut flour then dip in eggs and coat with flaked coconut.
5. Place coated shrimp into the air fryer basket.
6. Place the wire rack on LEVEL 2.
7. Select air fry mode set the temperature to 400 F and set time to 8 minutes. Press start to begin preheating.
8. Once the oven is preheated, place the air fry basket on the wire rack and close the oven door to start cooking.
9. Cook for 8 minutes.
10. Serve and enjoy.

Nutritional Value (Amount per Serving):

- Calories 115
- Fat 4.8 g
- Carbohydrates 5.1 g
- Sugar 0.7 g
- Protein 12.9 g
- Cholesterol 122 mg

Crab Cakes

Preparation Time: 10 minutes
Cooking Time: 30 minutes
Serve: 6

Ingredients:

- 15 oz lump crab meat
- 1 tsp old bay seasoning
- 1 tsp mustard
- 2/3 cup mashed avocado
- 1/4 cup onion, diced
- 1 cup crushed crackers

Directions:

1. Add all ingredients into the bowl and mix until just combined.
2. Make patties from the mixture and place onto the sheet pan.
3. Place the wire rack on LEVEL 2.
4. Select bake mode set the temperature to 350 F and set time to 30 minutes. Press start to begin preheating.
5. Once the oven is preheated, place a sheet pan on a wire rack and close the oven door to start cooking.
6. Cook for 30 minutes.
7. Serve and enjoy.

Nutritional Value (Amount per Serving):

- Calories 156
- Fat 12 g
- Carbohydrates 12 g
- Sugar 2 g
- Protein 12 g
- Cholesterol 42 mg

Air Fryer Scallops

Preparation Time: 10 minutes
Cooking Time: 4 minutes
Serve: 4

Ingredients:

- 16 scallops
- 1/4 tsp garlic powder
- 1 tsp olive oil
- Pepper
- Salt

Directions:

1. Add scallops and remaining ingredients into the mixing bowl and toss well.
2. Add scallops to the air fryer basket.
3. Place the wire rack on LEVEL 2.
4. Select air fry mode set the temperature to 390 F and set time to 4 minutes. Press start to begin preheating.
5. Once the oven is preheated, place the air fry basket on the wire rack and close the oven door to start cooking.
6. Cook for 4 minutes.
7. Serve and enjoy.

Nutritional Value (Amount per Serving):

- Calories 116
- Fat 2 g
- Carbohydrates 3 g
- Sugar 0 g
- Protein 20 g
- Cholesterol 40 mg

Chapter 6: Vegetables & Side Dishes

Crispy Brussels Sprouts

Preparation Time: 10 minutes
Cooking Time: 10 minutes
Serve: 2

Ingredients:

- 2 cups Brussels sprouts, sliced
- 1 tbsp olive oil
- 1 tbsp vinegar
- 1/4 tsp sea salt

Directions:

1. Add all ingredients into the large bowl and toss well.
2. Transfer Brussels sprouts into the air fryer basket.
3. Place the wire rack on LEVEL 2.
4. Select air fry mode set the temperature to 400 F and set time to 10 minutes. Press start to begin preheating.
5. Once the oven is preheated, place the air fry basket on the wire rack and close the oven door to start cooking.
6. Cook for 10 minutes.
7. Serve and enjoy.

Nutritional Value (Amount per Serving):

- Calories 100
- Fat 7.3 g
- Carbohydrates 8.1 g
- Sugar 1.9 g
- Protein 3 g
- Cholesterol 0 mg

Air Fryer Eggplant

Preparation Time: 10 minutes
Cooking Time: 12 minutes
Serve: 2

Ingredients:

- 1 eggplant, washed and cubed
- 1/4 tsp oregano
- 1 tbsp olive oil
- 1/2 tsp garlic powder

Directions:

1. Add all ingredients into the mixing bowl and toss well.
2. Transfer eggplant mixture into the air fryer basket.
3. Place the wire rack on LEVEL 2.
4. Select air fry mode set the temperature to 390 F and set time to 12 minutes. Press start to begin preheating.
5. Once the oven is preheated, place the air fry basket on the wire rack and close the oven door to start cooking.
6. Cook for 12 minutes.
7. Serve and enjoy.

Nutritional Value (Amount per Serving):

- Calories 120
- Fat 7.4 g
- Carbohydrates 14.1 g
- Sugar 7.1 g
- Protein 2.4 g
- Cholesterol 0 mg

Healthy Sliced Mushrooms

Preparation Time: 10 minutes
Cooking Time: 12 minutes
Serve: 2

Ingredients:

- 8 oz mushrooms, sliced
- 1/2 tsp garlic powder
- 1 tbsp olive oil
- 1 tbsp parsley, chopped
- 1 tsp soy sauce
- Pepper
- Salt

Directions:

1. Add all ingredients into the bowl and toss well.
2. Transfer mushrooms to the air fryer basket.
3. Place the wire rack on LEVEL 2.
4. Select air fry mode set the temperature to 380 F and set time to 12 minutes. Press start to begin preheating.
5. Once the oven is preheated, place the air fry basket on the wire rack and close the oven door to start cooking.
6. Cook for 12 minutes.
7. Serve and enjoy.

Nutritional Value (Amount per Serving):

- Calories 89
- Fat 7.4 g
- Carbohydrates 4.6 g
- Sugar 2.2 g
- Protein 3.9 g
- Cholesterol 0 mg

Flavorful Air Fryer Okra

Preparation Time: 10 minutes
Cooking Time: 12 minutes
Serve: 1

Ingredients:

- 1/2 lb okra, ends trimmed and sliced
- 1/2 tsp ground coriander
- 1/2 tsp ground cumin
- 1 tsp olive oil
- 1/2 tsp mango powder
- 1/2 tsp chili powder
- 1/8 tsp pepper
- 1/4 tsp salt

Directions:

1. Add all ingredients into the large bowl and toss well.
2. Transfer okra mixture into the air fryer basket.
3. Place the wire rack on LEVEL 2.
4. Select air fry mode set the temperature to 350 F and set time to 12 minutes. Press start to begin preheating.
5. Once the oven is preheated, place the air fry basket on the wire rack and close the oven door to start cooking.
6. Cook for 12 minutes.
7. Serve and enjoy.

Nutritional Value (Amount per Serving):

- Calories 139
- Fat 5.6 g
- Carbohydrates 18.3 g
- Sugar 3.5 g
- Protein 4.8 g
- Cholesterol 0 mg

Parmesan Broccoli Florets

Preparation Time: 10 minutes
Cooking Time: 5 minutes
Serve: 2

Ingredients:

- 3 cups broccoli florets
- 2 garlic cloves, minced
- 1/4 cup parmesan cheese, grated
- 2 tbsp olive oil

Directions:

1. Add all ingredients into the large bowl and toss well.
2. Transfer broccoli mixture into the air fryer basket.
3. Place the wire rack on LEVEL 2.
4. Select air fry mode set the temperature to 360 F and set time to 5 minutes. Press start to begin preheating.
5. Once the oven is preheated, place the air fry basket on the wire rack and close the oven door to start cooking.
6. Cook for 10 minutes.

Nutritional Value (Amount per Serving):

- Calories 171
- Fat 14 g
- Carbohydrates 10 g
- Sugar 2.4 g
- Protein 4 g
- Cholesterol 0 mg

Zucchini Patties

Preparation Time: 10 minutes
Cooking Time: 25 minutes
Serve: 6

Ingredients:

- 1 egg, lightly beaten
- 1 cup zucchini, shredded
- 2 tbsp onion, minced
- 1/4 cup parmesan cheese, grated
- 1/2 tbsp Dijon mustard
- 1/2 tbsp mayonnaise
- 1/2 cup breadcrumbs
- Pepper
- Salt

Directions:

1. Add all ingredients into the bowl and mix until well combined.
2. Make patties from the zucchini mixture and place it into the air fryer basket.
3. Place the wire rack on LEVEL 2.
4. Select air fry mode set the temperature to 400 F and set time to 25 minutes. Press start to begin preheating.
5. Once the oven is preheated, place the air fry basket on the wire rack and close the oven door to start cooking.
6. Cook for 25 minutes.
7. Serve and enjoy.

Nutritional Value (Amount per Serving):

- Calories 81
- Fat 3.2 g
- Carbohydrates 7.9 g
- Sugar 1.2 g
- Protein 4.5 g
- Cholesterol 33 mg

Sweet Potato Fries

Preparation Time: 10 minutes
Cooking Time: 16 minutes
Serve: 2

Ingredients:

- 2 sweet potatoes, peeled and cut into fries
- 1/4 tsp garlic powder
- 1 tbsp olive oil
- 1/2 tsp chili powder
- Salt

Directions:

1. In a large bowl, add sweet potato fries, garlic powder, chili powder, olive oil, and salt and toss until well coated.
2. Add sweet potato fries into the air fryer basket.
3. Place the wire rack on LEVEL 2.
4. Select air fry mode set the temperature to 380 F and set time to 16 minutes. Press start to begin preheating.
5. Once the oven is preheated, place the air fry basket on the wire rack and close the oven door to start cooking.
6. Cook for 15 minutes.
7. Serve and enjoy.

Nutritional Value (Amount per Serving):

- Calories 119
- Fat 7.1 g
- Carbohydrates 13 g
- Sugar 2.9 g
- Protein 1.2 g
- Cholesterol 0 mg

Baked Vegetables

Preparation Time: 10 minutes
Cooking Time: 35 minutes
Serve: 4

Ingredients:

- 3 cups Brussels sprouts, cut in half
- 8 oz mushrooms, cut in half
- 2 bell peppers, cut into 2-inch chunks
- 1 tsp thyme
- 2 tbsp vinegar
- 1 onion, cut into wedges
- 2 zucchini, cut into 1/2-inch thick half circles
- 1/4 cup olive oil
- 1/2 tsp salt

Directions:

1. Line sheet pan with parchment paper and set aside.
2. Add vegetables into the zip-lock bag.
3. Mix together thyme, vinegar, oil, and salt and pour over vegetables.
4. Seal zip-lock bag and shake well and place it in the refrigerator for 1 hour.
5. Spread marinated vegetables on a sheet pan.
6. Place the wire rack on LEVEL 2.
7. Select bake mode set the temperature to 375 F and set time to 35 minutes. Press start to begin preheating.
8. Once the oven is preheated, place the pan on a wire rack and close the oven door to start cooking.
9. Cook for 35 minutes.
10. Serve and enjoy.

Nutritional Value (Amount per Serving):

- Calories 195
- Fat 13.4 g
- Carbohydrates 18.4 g
- Sugar 8.3 g
- Protein 6.1 g
- Cholesterol 0 mg

Baked Honey Balsamic Vegetables

Preparation Time: 10 minutes
Cooking Time: 30 minutes
Serve: 3

Ingredients:

- 1 cup sweet potato, cut into chunks
- 1 cup broccoli, cut into chunks
- 1 tbsp honey
- 1 tbsp balsamic vinegar
- 1 cup mushrooms, sliced
- 1 cup beet, cut into chunks
- 1 tbsp olive oil
- Pepper
- Salt

Directions:

1. Line sheet pan with parchment paper and set aside.
2. In a bowl, toss vegetables with oil, pepper, and salt.
3. Spread vegetables on a sheet pan.
4. Place the wire rack on LEVEL 2.
5. Select bake mode set the temperature to 390 F and set time to 25 minutes. Press start to begin preheating.
6. Once the oven is preheated, place the pan on a wire rack and close the oven door to start cooking.
7. Cook for 25 minutes.
8. Once vegetables are baked then mix honey and vinegar and drizzle over vegetables and bake for 5 minutes more.
9. Serve and enjoy.

Nutritional Value (Amount per Serving):

- Calories 165
- Fat 5.1 g
- Carbohydrates 28 g
- Sugar 15.1 g
- Protein 3.9 g
- Cholesterol 0 mg

Vegetable Casserole

Preparation Time: 10 minutes
Cooking Time: 1 hour 15 minutes
Serve: 12

Ingredients:

- 16 oz broccoli florets
- 16 oz cauliflower florets
- 8 oz mozzarella cheese, grated
- 8 oz cheddar cheese, grated
- 2 eggs, lightly beaten
- 1 onion, diced
- 1 cup mayonnaise
- 8 oz can bean sprouts, drained
- 8 oz can water chestnuts, drained and sliced
- 10.5 oz cream of mushroom soup
- Pepper
- Salt

Directions:

1. Spray a 9*13-inch baking dish with cooking spray and set aside.
2. In a bowl, mix together mayonnaise, onions, eggs, soup, pepper, and salt.
3. Add broccoli, cauliflower, water chestnuts, and bean sprouts into the baking dish.
4. Pour mayonnaise mixture over vegetable mixture. Sprinkle with mozzarella cheese and cheddar cheese.
5. Place the wire rack on LEVEL 2.
6. Select bake mode, set the temperature to 350 F, and set time to 1 hour 15 minutes. Press start to begin preheating.
7. Once the oven is preheated, place the pan on a wire rack and close the oven door to start cooking.
8. Cook for 75 minutes.
9. Serve and enjoy.

Nutritional Value (Amount per Serving):

- Calories 260
- Fat 17.8 g
- Carbohydrates 13.2 g
- Sugar 4.5 g
- Protein 14 g
- Cholesterol 62 mg

Chapter 7: Snacks & Appetizers

Tasty Sweet Potato Bites

Preparation Time: 10 minutes
Cooking Time: 45 minutes
Serve: 6

Ingredients:

- 2 lbs sweet potatoes, peel and cut into 1/2-inch cubes
- 1/2 tsp chili powder
- 1/2 tsp cinnamon
- 2 tbsp olive oil
- 1/2 tsp onion powder
- 1/2 tsp garlic powder
- Pepper
- Salt

Directions:

1. Spray sheet pan with cooking spray and set aside.
2. Spread sweet potato on a sheet pan.
3. Drizzle with oil and season with spices. Toss to coat.
4. Place the wire rack on LEVEL 2.
5. Select bake mode set the temperature to 400 F and set time to 45 minutes. Press start to begin preheating.
6. Once the oven is preheated, place a sheet pan on a wire rack and close the oven door to start cooking.
7. Cook for 45 minutes.
8. Serve and enjoy.

Nutritional Value (Amount per Serving):

- Calories 221
- Fat 5 g
- Carbohydrates 42.8 g
- Sugar 0.9 g
- Protein 2.4 g
- Cholesterol 0 mg

Potato Croquettes

Preparation Time: 10 minutes
Cooking Time: 60 minutes
Serve: 6

Ingredients:

- 2 cups sweet potatoes, mashed
- 2 cups quinoa, cooked
- 1/4 cup celery, diced
- 1/4 cup scallions, chopped
- 1/4 cup parsley, chopped
- 1/4 cup flour
- 2 tsp Italian seasoning
- 2 garlic cloves, minced
- Pepper
- Salt

Directions:

1. Spray sheet pan with cooking spray and set aside.
2. Add all ingredients into the large bowl and mix well.
3. Make 1-inch round croquettes from mixture and place on a sheet pan.
4. Place the wire rack on LEVEL 2.
5. Select bake mode set the temperature to 375 F, and set time to 60 minutes. Press start to begin preheating.
6. Once the oven is preheated, place a sheet pan on a wire rack and close the oven door to start cooking.
7. Cook for 60 minutes.
8. Serve and enjoy.

Nutritional Value (Amount per Serving):

- Calories 296
- Fat 4.1 g
- Carbohydrates 55.4 g
- Sugar 0.6 g
- Protein 9.6 g
- Cholesterol 1 mg

Healthy Broccoli Patties

Preparation Time: 10 minutes
Cooking Time: 30 minutes
Serve: 4

Ingredients:

- 2 eggs, lightly beaten
- 2 cups mozzarella cheese, shredded
- 1/4 cup breadcrumbs
- 1 tsp garlic, minced
- 3 cups broccoli florets, steam & chopped
- Pepper
- Salt

Directions:

1. Add all ingredients into the large bowl and mix until well combined.
2. Make patties from mixture and place it on the parchment-lined sheet pan.
3. Place the wire rack on LEVEL 2.
4. Select bake mode set the temperature to 375 F and set time to 30 minutes. Press start to begin preheating.
5. Once the oven is preheated, place a sheet pan on a wire rack and close the oven door to start cooking.
6. Cook for 30 minutes.
7. Serve and enjoy.

Nutritional Value (Amount per Serving):

- Calories 327
- Fat 24.5 g
- Carbohydrates 7.4 g
- Sugar 1.6 g
- Protein 20.4 g
- Cholesterol 141 mg

Parmesan Potatoes Wedges

Preparation Time: 10 minutes
Cooking Time: 45 minutes
Serve: 4

Ingredients:

- 5 potatoes, cut into wedges
- 2 thyme sprigs
- 1/2 cup parmesan cheese, grated
- 2 tbsp lemon juice
- 1/3 cup olive oil
- 2 garlic cloves, minced
- Pepper
- Salt

Directions:

1. Add potato wedges into the bowl.
2. Add lemon juice, oil, garlic, thyme, cheese, pepper, and salt and toss well.
3. Place potato wedges onto the sheet pan.
4. Place the wire rack on LEVEL 2.
5. Select bake mode set the temperature to 325 F and set time to 45 minutes. Press start to begin preheating.
6. Once the oven is preheated, place a sheet pan on a wire rack and close the oven door to start cooking.
7. Cook for 45 minutes.
8. Serve and enjoy.

Nutritional Value (Amount per Serving):

- Calories 369
- Fat 19.6 g
- Carbohydrates 43.2 g
- Sugar 3.3 g
- Protein 8.3 g
- Cholesterol 8 mg

Healthy Baked Almonds

Preparation Time: 10 minutes
Cooking Time: 20 minutes
Serve: 12

Ingredients:

- 2 1/2 cups almonds
- 1/4 tsp chili powder
- 1 tbsp fresh rosemary, chopped
- 1 tbsp olive oil
- 2 1/2 tbsp maple syrup
- 1/4 tsp cayenne
- 1/4 tsp ground coriander
- 1/4 tsp cumin
- Pinch of salt

Directions:

1. Spray sheet pan with cooking spray and set aside.
2. In a bowl, whisk oil, cayenne, coriander, cumin, chili powder, rosemary, maple syrup, and salt.
3. Add almond and stir to coat.
4. Spread almonds onto the prepared sheet pan.
5. Place the wire rack on LEVEL 2.
6. Select bake mode set the temperature to 325 F and set time to 20 minutes. Press start to begin preheating.
7. Once the oven is preheated, place a sheet pan on a wire rack and close the oven door to start cooking.
8. Cook for 20 minutes.
9. Serve and enjoy.

Nutritional Value (Amount per Serving):

- Calories 135
- Fat 11 g
- Carbohydrates 7.3 g
- Sugar 3.3 g
- Protein 4.2 g
- Cholesterol 0 mg

Parmesan Green Beans

Preparation Time: 10 minutes
Cooking Time: 15 minutes
Serve: 4

Ingredients:

- 1 lb green beans
- 1/4 tsp garlic powder
- 4 tbsp parmesan cheese
- 2 tbsp olive oil
- 1/4 tsp onion powder
- Pinch of salt

Directions:

1. Spray sheet pan with cooking spray and set aside.
2. Add green beans and remaining ingredients into the mixing bowl and toss well.
3. Arrange green beans onto the sheet pan.
4. Place the wire rack on LEVEL 2.
5. Select bake mode set the temperature to 400 F and set time to 15 minutes. Press start to begin preheating.
6. Once the oven is preheated, place a sheet pan on a wire rack and close the oven door to start cooking.
7. Cook for 15 minutes.
8. Serve and enjoy.

Nutritional Value (Amount per Serving):

- Calories 102
- Fat 7.5 g
- Carbohydrates 8.3 g
- Sugar 1.6 g
- Protein 2.6 g
- Cholesterol 1 mg

Cheesy Zucchini Chips

Preparation Time: 10 minutes
Cooking Time: 15 minutes
Serve: 8

Ingredients:

- 2 zucchini, sliced
- 3/4 cup parmesan cheese, grated
- 4 tbsp olive oil
- 1/2 tsp paprika
- 1/4 tsp garlic powder
- 1/4 tsp pepper
- Pinch of salt

Directions:

1. Spray sheet pan with cooking spray and set aside.
2. In a bowl, combine the oil, garlic powder, paprika, pepper, and salt.
3. Add sliced zucchini and toss to coat.
4. Arrange zucchini slices onto the sheet pan and sprinkle grated cheese on top.
5. Place the wire rack on LEVEL 2.
6. Select bake mode set the temperature to 375 F and set time to 15 minutes. Press start to begin preheating.
7. Once the oven is preheated, place a sheet pan on a wire rack and close the oven door to start cooking.
8. Cook for 15 minutes.
9. Serve and enjoy.

Nutritional Value (Amount per Serving):

- Calories 111
- Fat 9 g
- Carbohydrates 2.2 g
- Sugar 0.9 g
- Protein 4.4 g
- Cholesterol 7 mg

Healthy & Tasty Chickpeas

Preparation Time: 10 minutes
Cooking Time: 20 minutes
Serve: 4

Ingredients:

- 15 oz can chickpeas, drained, rinsed and pat dry
- 1/4 tsp paprika
- 1/4 tsp chili powder
- 1 tbsp olive oil
- 1/4 tsp pepper
- Pinch of salt

Directions:

1. Spray sheet pan with cooking spray and set aside.
2. Place the wire rack on LEVEL 2.
3. Select bake mode set the temperature to 450 F and set time to 25 minutes. Press start to begin preheating.
4. Once the oven is preheated, place the pan on a wire rack and close the oven door to start cooking.
5. Cook for 25 minutes.
6. Once chickpeas are done then immediately toss with chili powder, paprika, pepper, and salt.
7. Serve and enjoy.

Nutritional Value (Amount per Serving):

- Calories 155
- Fat 4.7 g
- Carbohydrates 24.2 g
- Sugar 0 g
- Protein 5.3 g
- Cholesterol 0 mg

Parmesan Cauliflower Florets

Preparation Time: 10 minutes
Cooking Time: 25 minutes
Serve: 4

Ingredients:

- 8 cups cauliflower florets
- 1/2 cup parmesan cheese, shredded
- 2 tbsp vinegar
- 1/4 tsp pepper
- 2 tbsp olive oil
- 1/4 tsp salt

Directions:

1. Spray sheet pan with cooking spray and set aside.
2. Toss cauliflower, oil, pepper, and salt. Toss well.
3. Spread cauliflower onto the sheet pan.
4. Place the wire rack on LEVEL 2.
5. Select bake mode set the temperature to 450 F, and set time to 20 minutes. Press start to begin preheating.
6. Once the oven is preheated, place the pan on a wire rack and close the oven door to start cooking.
7. Cook for 20 minutes.
8. Toss cauliflower with cheese and vinegar.
9. Return cauliflower to the oven and bake for 5 minutes more.
10. Serve and enjoy.

Nutritional Value (Amount per Serving):

- Calories 195
- Fat 13 g
- Carbohydrates 11 g
- Sugar 5 g
- Protein 11 g
- Cholesterol 14 mg

Healthy Zucchini Fries

Preparation Time: 10 minutes
Cooking Time: 30 minutes
Serve: 4

Ingredients:

- 1 egg
- 2 medium zucchini, cut into fries shape
- 1 cup parmesan cheese, grated
- 1 tsp Italian herbs
- 1 tsp garlic powder

Directions:

1. Preheat the oven to 425 F/ 218 C.
2. Spray a baking sheet pan with cooking spray and set aside.
3. In a small bowl, add egg and lightly whisk.
4. In a separate bowl, mix spices and parmesan cheese.
5. Dip zucchini fries in egg then coat with parmesan cheese mixture and place on a sheet pan.
6. Place the wire rack on LEVEL 2.
7. Select bake mode set the temperature to 425 F and set time to 30 minutes. Press start to begin preheating.
8. Once the oven is preheated, place a sheet pan on a wire rack and close the oven door to start cooking.
9. Cook for 30 minutes.
10. Serve and enjoy.

Nutritional Value (Amount per Serving):

- Calories 185
- Fat 10.3 g
- Carbohydrates 3.9 g
- Sugar 2 g
- Protein 14.7 g
- Cholesterol 71 mg

Chapter 8: Dehydrate

Pineapple Slices

Preparation Time: 10 minutes
Cooking Time: 14 hours
Serve: 12

Ingredients:

- 12 pineapple slices

Directions:

1. Select dehydrate mode.
2. Select 2 LEVEL then set time for 14 hours and set the temperature to 125 F.
3. Place pineapple slices in the air fry basket and place basket in the oven. Press start.

Nutritional Value (Amount per Serving):

- Calories 374
- Fat 0.9 g
- Carbohydrates 99 g

- Sugar 74.5 g
- Protein 4.1 g
- Cholesterol 0 mg

Apple Slices

Preparation Time: 10 minutes
Cooking Time: 8 hours
Serve: 4

Ingredients:

- 2 apple, cored and cut into 1/8-inch thick slices
- 1 tsp ground cinnamon

Directions:

1. Select dehydrate mode.
2. Select 2 LEVEL then set time for 8 hours and set the temperature to 145 F.
3. Place apple slices in the air fry basket and place basket in the oven.
4. Sprinkle cinnamon on top of apple slices.
5. Press start.

Nutritional Value (Amount per Serving):

- Calories 60
- Fat 0.2 g
- Carbohydrates 16 g
- Sugar 11.6 g
- Protein 0.3 g
- Cholesterol 0 mg

Pear Slices

Preparation Time: 10 minutes
Cooking Time: 5 hours
Serve: 4

Ingredients:

- 2 pears, cut into 1/4-inch thick slices

Directions:

1. Select dehydrate mode.
2. Select 2 LEVEL then set time for 5 hours and set the temperature to 160 F.
3. Place pear slices in the air fry basket and place basket in the oven. Press start.

Nutritional Value (Amount per Serving):

- Calories 61
- Fat 0.2 g
- Carbohydrates 16 g

- Sugar 10.2 g
- Protein 0.4 g
- Cholesterol 0 mg

Mango Slices

Preparation Time: 10 minutes

Cooking Time: 12 hours

Serve: 4

Ingredients:

- 2 large mangoes, peel, and cut into 1/4-inch thick slices

Directions:

1. Select dehydrate mode.
2. Select 2 LEVEL then set time for 12 hours and set the temperature to 135 F.
3. Place mango slices in the air fry basket and place basket in the oven. Press start.

Nutritional Value (Amount per Serving):

- Calories 102
- Fat 0.6 g
- Carbohydrates 25 g
- Sugar 23 g
- Protein 1.4 g
- Cholesterol 0 mg

Zucchini Slices

Preparation Time: 10 minutes
Cooking Time: 12 hours
Serve: 4

Ingredients:

- 1 zucchini, sliced thinly

Directions:

1. Select dehydrate mode.
2. Select 2 LEVEL then set time for 12 hours and set the temperature to 135 F.
3. Place zucchini slices in the air fry basket and place basket in the oven. Press start.

Nutritional Value (Amount per Serving):

- Calories 10
- Fat 0.1 g
- Carbohydrates 2.1 g
- Sugar 0.9 g
- Protein 0.6 g
- Cholesterol 0 mg

Dragon Fruit Slices

Preparation Time: 10 minutes
Cooking Time: 12 hours
Serve: 4

Ingredients:

- 2 dragon fruit, peel & cut into 1/4-inch thick slices

Directions:

1. Select dehydrate mode.
2. Select 2 LEVEL then set time for 12 hours and set the temperature to 115 F.
3. Place dragon fruit slices in the air fry basket and place basket in the oven. Press start.

Nutritional Value (Amount per Serving):

- Calories 25
- Fat 0 g
- Carbohydrates 6 g
- Sugar 6 g
- Protein 0 g
- Cholesterol 0 mg

Broccoli Florets

Preparation Time: 10 minutes
Cooking Time: 12 hours
Serve: 6

Ingredients:

- 1 lb broccoli florets
- Pepper
- Salt

Directions:

1. Select dehydrate mode.
2. Select 2 LEVEL then set time for 12 hours and set the temperature to 115 F.
3. Place broccoli florets in the air fry basket and place basket in the oven. Press start.

Nutritional Value (Amount per Serving):

- Calories 25
- Fat 0.3 g
- Carbohydrates 5 g
- Sugar 1.3 g
- Protein 2.1 g
- Cholesterol 0 mg

Avocado Slices

Preparation Time: 10 minutes
Cooking Time: 10 hours
Serve: 4

Ingredients:

- 4 avocados, halved and pitted

Directions:

1. Select dehydrate mode.
2. Select 2 LEVEL then set time for 10 hours and set the temperature to 160 F.
3. Place avocado slices in the air fry basket and place basket in the oven. Press start.

Nutritional Value (Amount per Serving):

- Calories 415
- Fat 39 g
- Carbohydrates 17.5 g
- Sugar 1.1 g
- Protein 3.9 g
- Cholesterol 0 mg

Sweet Potato Chips

Preparation Time: 10 minutes
Cooking Time: 12 hours
Serve: 2

Ingredients:

- 2 sweet potatoes, peel and sliced thinly
- 1 tsp olive oil
- 1/8 tsp cinnamon
- Salt

Directions:

1. Add sweet potato slices in a bowl. Add cinnamon, oil, and salt and toss well.
2. Select dehydrate mode.
3. Select 2 LEVEL then set time for 12 hours and set the temperature to 125 F.
4. Place sweet potato slices in the air fry basket and place basket in the oven. Press start.

Nutritional Value (Amount per Serving):

- Calories 195
- Fat 2 g
- Carbohydrates 41 g
- Sugar 0.8 g
- Protein 2.3 g
- Cholesterol 0 mg

Kiwi Chips

Preparation Time: 5 minutes
Cooking Time: 10 hours
Serve: 4

Ingredients:

- 6 kiwis, peeled & cut into 1/4-inch thick slices

Directions:

1. Select dehydrate mode.
2. Select 2 LEVEL then set time for 10 hours and set the temperature to 135 F.
3. Place kiwi slices in the air fry basket and place basket in the oven. Press start.

Nutritional Value (Amount per Serving):

- Calories 71
- Fat 0.6 g
- Carbohydrates 16 g
- Sugar 10.3 g
- Protein 1.3 g
- Cholesterol 0 mg

Chapter 9: Desserts

Moist & Fudgy Brownie

Preparation Time: 10 minutes
Cooking Time: 45 minutes
Serve: 16

Ingredients:

- 4 eggs
- 1 tsp vanilla
- 1 cup of chocolate chips
- 2 tsp baking powder
- 1 cup all-purpose flour
- 1 1/4 cups butter
- 1 1/2 cups cocoa powder
- 2 1/2 cups granulated sugar
- 1/2 tsp kosher salt

Directions:

1. Spray 9*9-inch cake pan with cooking spray and set aside.
2. Add butter, cocoa powder, and sugar in microwave-safe bowl and microwave for 1 minute. Stir until butter is melted.
3. Add eggs one by one and stir until well combined.
4. Add baking powder, flour, and salt and stir well. Add chocolate chips and fold well.
5. Pour batter into the prepared cake pan.
6. Place the wire rack on LEVEL 2.
7. Select bake mode set the temperature to 325 F and set time to 45 minutes. Press start to begin preheating.
8. Once the oven is preheated, place the cake pan on a wire rack and close the oven door to start cooking.
9. Cook for 45 minutes.
10. Slice and serve.

Nutritional Value (Amount per Serving):

- Calories 364
- Fat 19 g
- Carbohydrates 48 g
- Sugar 36 g
- Protein 4 g
- Cholesterol 81 mg

Vanilla Cupcake

Preparation Time: 10 minutes
Cooking Time: 20 minutes
Serve: 12

Ingredients:

- 3 eggs
- 1/2 cup butter
- 1/4 cup milk
- 1 tsp vanilla
- 2/3 cup sugar
- 1 1/2 tsp baking powder
- 1 1/2 cups all-purpose flour
- 1/4 tsp salt

Directions:

1. Line the muffin pan with cupcake liners and set aside.
2. In a bowl, mix flour, salt, and baking powder and set aside.
3. In a separate bowl, beat the sugar and butter until fluffy.
4. Add eggs one by one and beat until well combined.
5. Add flour mixture and beat until well combined.
6. Add milk, vanilla, and remaining flour mixture and beat until fully incorporated.
7. Pour mixture into the prepared muffin pan.
8. Place the wire rack on LEVEL 2.
9. Select bake mode set the temperature to 350 F, and set time to 20 minutes. Press start to begin preheating.
10. Once the oven is preheated, place the muffin pan on the wire rack and close the oven door to start cooking.
11. Cook for 20 minutes.
12. Serve and enjoy.

Nutritional Value (Amount per Serving):

- Calories 186
- Fat 9 g
- Carbohydrates 23 g
- Sugar 11.5 g
- Protein 3.2 g
- Cholesterol 62 mg

Pumpkin Muffins

Preparation Time: 10 minutes
Cooking Time: 35 minutes
Serve: 12

Ingredients:

- 2 eggs
- 1 tsp baking soda
- 1/2 cup of chocolate chips
- 2 cups flour
- 1 cup can pumpkin puree
- 1/2 cup olive oil
- 1 tsp pumpkin pie spice
- 1/2 cup maple syrup
- 1/2 tsp salt

Directions:

1. Line the muffin pan with cupcake liners and set aside.
2. In a large bowl, mix flour, baking soda, spice, and salt.
3. In a separate bowl, whisk eggs, pumpkin puree, oil, and maple syrup.
4. Slowly add dry mixture to the wet mixture and mix well.
5. Add choco chips and fold well.
6. Pour batter into prepared muffin pan.
7. Place the wire rack on LEVEL 2.
8. Select bake mode set the temperature to 350 F and set time to 35 minutes. Press start to begin preheating.
9. Once the oven is preheated, place the pan on a wire rack and close the oven door to start cooking.
10. Cook for 35 minutes.
11. Serve and enjoy.

Nutritional Value (Amount per Serving):

- Calories 234
- Fat 11.5 g
- Carbohydrates 29 g
- Sugar 11.9 g
- Protein 3.7 g
- Cholesterol 29 mg

Delicious Strawberry Bars

Preparation Time: 10 minutes
Cooking Time: 30 minutes
Serve: 16

Ingredients:

- 3/4 cup strawberry preserves
- 1 tsp vanilla
- 10 tbsp butter, melted
- 1 tsp baking soda
- 1 tsp xanthan gum
- 3/4 cup brown sugar
- 1 cup rolled oats
- 1 cup flour
- 1/4 tsp salt

Directions:

1. Spray baking dish with cooking spray and set aside.
2. In a large bowl, mix flour, oats, xanthan gum, brown sugar, baking soda, and salt.
3. Add butter and vanilla to flour mixture and stir well to combine.
4. Set aside 1/3 of the flour mixture.
5. Transfer the remaining mixture to the prepared baking dish and press down with a spatula.
6. Spread strawberry preserves on top.
7. Spread remaining flour mixture over the strawberry layer.
8. Place the wire rack on LEVEL 2.
9. Select bake mode set the temperature to 350 F and set time to 30 minutes. Press start to begin preheating.
10. Once the oven is preheated, place the baking dish on a wire rack and close the oven door to start cooking.
11. Cook for 30 minutes.
12. Slice and serve.

Nutritional Value (Amount per Serving):

- Calories 180
- Fat 7.6 g
- Carbohydrates 26 g
- Sugar 14 g
- Protein 1.6 g
- Cholesterol 19 mg

Simple Ricotta Cake

Preparation Time: 10 minutes
Cooking Time: 55 minutes
Serve: 8

Ingredients:

- 4 eggs
- 18 oz ricotta cheese
- 1 fresh lemon zest
- 2 tbsp stevia
- 1 fresh lemon juice

Directions:

1. In a large bowl, whisk the ricotta with an electric mixer until smooth.
2. Add egg one by one and whisk well.
3. Add lemon juice, lemon zest, and stevia and mix well.
4. Transfer mixture into the prepared cake pan.
5. Place the wire rack on LEVEL 2.
6. Select bake mode set the temperature to 350 F and set time to 55 minutes. Press start to begin preheating.
7. Once the oven is preheated, place the cake pan on a wire rack and close the oven door to start cooking.
8. Cook for 55 minutes.
9. Place cake in the refrigerator for 1-2 hours.
10. Cut into the slices and serve.

Nutritional Value (Amount per Serving):

- Calories 121
- Fat 7.1 g
- Carbohydrates 5 g
- Sugar 1.1 g
- Protein 10 g
- Cholesterol 101 mg

Coconut Almond Cake

Preparation Time: 10 minutes
Cooking Time: 40 minutes
Serve: 16

Ingredients:

- 4 eggs
- 1 tsp baking powder
- 2 tsp vanilla
- 1/3 cup Swerve
- 2 oz cream cheese, softened
- 2 tbsp butter
- Pinch of salt
- 1 cup almond flour
- 1/2 cup coconut flour
- 4 oz half and half

For topping:

- 1 cup almonds, toasted and sliced
- 1/3 cup Swerve
- 6 tbsp butter, melted
- 1 cup almond flour

Directions:

1. Spray an 8-inch cake pan with cooking spray and set aside.
2. Add all ingredients except topping ingredients into the large bowl and mix with an electric mixer.
3. Pour batter into the prepared cake pan and spread evenly.
4. Mix together all topping ingredients until it looks like crumble.
5. Sprinkle topping mixture evenly on top of batter.
6. Place the wire rack on LEVEL 2.
7. Select bake mode set the temperature to 350 F and set time to 40 minutes. Press start to begin preheating.
8. Once the oven is preheated, place the cake pan on a wire rack and close the oven door to start cooking.
9. Cook for 40 minutes.
10. Cut into the slices and serve.

Nutritional Value (Amount per Serving):

- Calories 210
- Fat 19.5 g
- Carbohydrates 5 g

- Sugar 0.7 g
- Protein 6 g
- Cholesterol 63 mg

Apple Bars

Preparation Time: 10 minutes
Cooking Time: 45 minutes
Serve: 8

Ingredients:

- 1/4 cup dried apples
- 1 tbsp ground flax seed
- 2 tbsp swerve
- 1/4 cup coconut butter, softened
- 1 cup pecans
- 1 cup of water
- 1 tsp vanilla
- 1 1/2 tsp baking powder
- 1 1/2 tsp cinnamon

Directions:

1. Spray 8*8 square baking dish with cooking spray and set aside.
2. Add all ingredients into the blender and blend until smooth.
3. Pour blended mixture into the baking dish.
4. Place the wire rack on LEVEL 2.
5. Select bake mode set the temperature to 350 F and set time to 45 minutes. Press start to begin preheating.
6. Once the oven is preheated, place the baking dish on a wire rack and close the oven door to start cooking.
7. Cook for 45 minutes.
8. Cut into pieces and serve.

Nutritional Value (Amount per Serving):

- Calories 161
- Fat 14.8 g
- Carbohydrates 6.3 g
- Sugar 1.8 g
- Protein 2.2 g
- Cholesterol 0 mg

Pecan Cookies

Preparation Time: 15 minutes
Cooking Time: 20 minutes
Serve: 16

Ingredients:

- 1 cup pecans
- 1 tsp vanilla
- 1/3 cup coconut flour
- 1 cup almond flour
- 1/2 cup butter
- 2 tsp gelatin
- 2/3 cup Swerve

Directions:

1. Spray sheet pan with cooking spray and set aside.
2. Add butter, vanilla, gelatin, swerve, coconut flour, and almond flour into the food processor and process until crumbs form.
3. Add pecans and process until chopped.
4. Make cookies from the prepared mixture and place onto a sheet pan.
5. Place the wire rack on LEVEL 3.
6. Select bake mode set the temperature to 350 F and set time to 20 minutes. Press start to begin preheating.
7. Once the oven is preheated, place a sheet pan on a wire rack and close the oven door to start cooking.
8. Cook for 20 minutes.
9. Serve and enjoy.

Nutritional Value (Amount per Serving):

- Calories 115
- Fat 11.7 g
- Carbohydrates 1.7 g
- Sugar 0.4 g
- Protein 1.2 g
- Cholesterol 15 mg

Easy Pumpkin Cookies

Preparation Time: 10 minutes
Cooking Time: 25 minutes
Serve: 27

Ingredients:

- 1 egg
- 1 tsp liquid stevia
- 1/2 cup butter
- 1/2 cup pumpkin puree
- 2 cups almond flour
- 1/2 tsp pumpkin pie spice
- 1/2 tsp baking powder
- 1 tsp vanilla

Directions:

1. Spray sheet pan with cooking spray and set aside.
2. In a large bowl, add all ingredients and mix until well combined.
3. Make cookies from mixture and place onto a prepared sheet pan.
4. Place the wire rack on LEVEL 3.
5. Select bake mode set the temperature to 300 F and set time to 25 minutes. Press start to begin preheating.
6. Once the oven is preheated, place a sheet pan on a wire rack and close the oven door to start cooking.
7. Cook for 25 minutes.
8. Serve and enjoy.

Nutritional Value (Amount per Serving):

- Calories 46
- Fat 4.6 g
- Carbohydrates 0.9 g
- Sugar 0.3 g
- Protein 0.7 g
- Cholesterol 15 mg

Blueberry Muffins

Preparation Time: 10 minutes
Cooking Time: 25 minutes
Serve: 8

Ingredients:

- 4 eggs
- 1/2 cup blueberries
- 1 tsp vanilla
- 1/2 cup heavy whipping cream
- 1/2 cup butter, melted
- 1 tsp baking powder
- 3 tbsp swerve
- 2 cups almond flour
- 1 tbsp lemon juice

Directions:

1. Line the muffin pan with cupcake liners and set aside.
2. In a large bowl, whisk eggs with lemon juice, vanilla, heavy whipping cream, and butter.
3. In a separate bowl, mix together almond flour, swerve, and baking powder.
4. Add almond flour mixture to the egg mixture and mix until well combined. Add blueberries and fold well.
5. Pour batter into a prepared muffin pan.
6. Place the wire rack on LEVEL 2.
7. Select bake mode set the temperature to 350 F and set time to 25 minutes. Press start to begin preheating.
8. Once the oven is preheated, place the muffin pan on the wire rack and close the oven door to start cooking.
9. Cook for 25 minutes.
10. Serve and enjoy.

Nutritional Value (Amount per Serving):

- Calories 329
- Fat 30.5 g
- Carbohydrates 8.9 g
- Sugar 2.2 g
- Protein 9.1 g
- Cholesterol 123 mg

Chapter 10: 30-Day Meal Plan

Day 1

Breakfast- Mushroom Zucchini Frittata

Lunch- Rosemary Basil Salmon

Dinner- Crispy Crusted Pork Chops

Day 2

Breakfast- Feta Spinach Frittata

Lunch- Juicy Turkey Breast

Dinner- Asian Lamb

Day 3

Breakfast- Breakfast Mushroom Quiche

Lunch- Delicious White Fish Fillet

Dinner- Flavorful Marinated Steak

Day 4

Breakfast- Italian Egg Muffins

Lunch- Delicious Turkey Patties

Dinner- Crispy Parmesan Pork Chops

Day 5

Breakfast- Feta Zucchini Muffins

Lunch- Italian Salmon

Dinner- Juicy Pork Chops

Day 6

Breakfast- Healthy Baked Vegetable Quiche

Lunch- Chicken Zucchini Patties

Dinner- Tender Pork Chops

Day 7

Breakfast- Nutritious Tuna Muffins

Lunch- Dijon Salmon

Dinner- Pesto Pork Chops

Day 8

Breakfast- Tomato Frittata

Lunch- Rosemary Garlic Turkey Breast

Dinner- Delicious Baked Pork Ribs

Day 9

Breakfast- Baked Omelet

Lunch- Blackened Fish Fillets

Dinner- Beef Tips

Day 10

Breakfast- Sausage Veggie Egg Bake

Lunch- Herb Turkey Breast

Dinner- Vegetable Casserole

Day 11

Breakfast- Cheesy Baked Ham Omelet

Lunch- Lemon Pepper Fish Fillets

Dinner- Baked Honey Balsamic Vegetables

Day 12

Breakfast- Healthy Berry Oatmeal

Lunch- Adobo Chicken

Dinner- Baked Vegetables

Day 13

Breakfast- Kale Zucchini Bake

Lunch- Tasty Shrimp Fajitas

Dinner- Baked Chicken Thighs

Day 14

Breakfast- Mixed Veggie Muffins

Lunch- Crispy Chicken Wings

Dinner- Honey Mustard Chicken

Day 15

Breakfast- Cinnamon Oatmeal Cake

Lunch- Rosemary Garlic Shrimp

Dinner- Chicken Thighs & Potatoes

Day 16

Breakfast- Mushroom Zucchini Frittata

Lunch- Rosemary Basil Salmon

Dinner- Crispy Crusted Pork Chops

Day 17

Breakfast- Feta Spinach Frittata

Lunch- Juicy Turkey Breast

Dinner- Asian Lamb

Day 18

Breakfast- Breakfast Mushroom Quiche

Lunch- Delicious White Fish Fillet

Dinner- Flavorful Marinated Steak

Day 19

Breakfast- Italian Egg Muffins

Lunch- Delicious Turkey Patties

Dinner- Crispy Parmesan Pork Chops

Day 20

Breakfast- Feta Zucchini Muffins

Lunch- Italian Salmon

Dinner- Juicy Pork Chops

Day 21

Breakfast- Healthy Baked Vegetable Quiche

Lunch- Chicken Zucchini Patties

Dinner- Tender Pork Chops

Day 22

Breakfast- Nutritious Tuna Muffins

Lunch- Dijon Salmon

Dinner- Pesto Pork Chops

Day 23

Breakfast- Tomato Frittata

Lunch- Rosemary Garlic Turkey Breast

Dinner- Delicious Baked Pork Ribs

Day 24

Breakfast- Baked Omelet

Lunch- Blackened Fish Fillets

Dinner- Beef Tips

Day 25

Breakfast- Sausage Veggie Egg Bake

Lunch- Herb Turkey Breast

Dinner- Vegetable Casserole

Day 26

Breakfast- Cheesy Baked Ham Omelet

Lunch- Lemon Pepper Fish Fillets

Dinner- Baked Honey Balsamic Vegetables

Day 27

Breakfast- Healthy Berry Oatmeal

Lunch- Adobo Chicken

Dinner- Baked Vegetables

Day 28

Breakfast- Kale Zucchini Bake

Lunch- Tasty Shrimp Fajitas

Dinner- Baked Chicken Thighs

Day 29

Breakfast- Mixed Veggie Muffins

Lunch- Crispy Chicken Wings

Dinner- Honey Mustard Chicken

Day 30

Breakfast- Cinnamon Oatmeal Cake

Lunch- Rosemary Garlic Shrimp

Dinner- Chicken Thighs & Potatoes

Conclusion

The Ninja Foodi XL Pro Air Oven is designed to cook a large portion of foods in a single cooking cycle. It is basically the combination of three different cooking techniques such as air fryer, toaster, and oven. The Ninja foodi XL oven has a multi-functional appliance capable to perform 10 1 cooking operations like air roast, air fry, whole roast, broil, reheat, toast, bake, dehydrate, bagel and pizza. The display comes with a big handle design offers a simple and user-friendly interface.

The book includes 100 different types of recipes like breakfast, poultry, beef, pork and lamb, fish and seafood, vegetables & side dishes, snacks & appetizer, dehydrate, and desserts. All the recipes written in this book are unique and written in an easily understandable form. The recipes are written in the standard format with their perfect preparation and cooking time followed by step by step cooking instructions. All the recipes end with their nutritional value information.

CPSIA information can be obtained
at www.ICGtesting.com
Printed in the USA
LVHW062007140821
695341LV00005B/311